The Power of Algorithms

How Computers Solve Problems Step by Step

IntelliGloss AI Education Series

By

Susie Hala

Legal Disclaimer

Educational Purpose Disclaimer

"This publication is part of the IntelliGloss AI Education Series, a structured curriculum support system for AI literacy in grades 6–12."

The information presented in this publication is provided for educational and informational purposes only. This book is intended to support educators, administrators, parents, and learners in understanding the concepts, opportunities, and challenges associated with artificial intelligence in education. It is not intended to serve as legal, technical, policy, cybersecurity, or professional advice.

Readers should consult qualified professionals, institutional guidelines, and local regulations before implementing any educational programs, technologies, or policies described in this book.

Technology and Accuracy Disclaimer
Artificial intelligence is a rapidly evolving field. While every effort has been made to ensure the accuracy and reliability of the information presented at the time of publication, technologies, policies, research findings, and best practices may change over time. The author and publisher make no guarantees that all information will remain current or applicable in future technological environments.

Readers are encouraged to verify tools, platforms, and recommendations independently before using them in educational settings.

Implementation Responsibility
Schools, educators, and institutions are solely responsible for determining how and whether to implement artificial intelligence tools, strategies, or classroom activities discussed in this book. Educational environments vary widely, and policies regarding technology use, student privacy, and curriculum development differ by district, state, and country.

The author and publisher assume no responsibility for outcomes resulting from the implementation of ideas, examples, or frameworks described in this book.

Student Safety and Data Privacy
Artificial intelligence tools may involve the collection or processing of data. Educators and institutions are responsible for ensuring that any technology used complies with applicable student privacy laws, data protection regulations, and school policies, including but not limited to FERPA, COPPA, GDPR, or other relevant regulations depending on jurisdiction.

The author and publisher are not responsible for the privacy practices, security policies, or data handling procedures of third-party platforms or software mentioned in this book.

Title: The Power of Algorithm How Computers Solve Problems Step by Step

ISBN: 978-1-972925-07-2

schools, and institutions are responsible for evaluating and implementing technologies in accordance with their own policies, legal requirements, and educational standards.

Cover design and layout by IntelliGloss Press
First Edition
2026

Printed in the United States of America

Dedication

This book is dedicated to the next generation of learners—
the students who will grow up in a world shaped by intelligent technology,
and who deserve to understand it with clarity, confidence, and purpose.

To the educators who show up every day with dedication and heart,
guiding students through a rapidly changing world—
your role has never been more important.

To the parents and families who support learning at home,
encouraging curiosity, responsibility, and growth—
you are the foundation of every child's success.

And to my granddaughters,
whose curiosity, imagination, and future inspire me to do this work—
this book is for you.

May you not only learn how to use technology,
but understand it, question it, and shape it for the good of others.

About the Author

Susie Hala
Founder of the IntelliGloss AI Education Series

Susie Hala is an author, educator, and curriculum developer dedicated to advancing artificial intelligence literacy in education. Her work focuses on helping schools, educators, and students understand how intelligent technologies are shaping modern society—and why that understanding is essential for the next generation.

Hala is the creator of the IntelliGloss AI Education Series, a comprehensive and growing collection of educational books designed to make complex artificial intelligence concepts accessible, structured, and practical for classroom use. Her work emphasizes clarity, organization, and responsible implementation, enabling schools to introduce AI literacy without requiring advanced technical backgrounds.

In addition to her work in education, Hala brings hands-on experience working with artificial intelligence systems, including early exposure to rule-based AI technologies during her time working with AT&T. She has also developed modern digital platforms that integrate artificial intelligence, automation, and online systems, building e-commerce solutions and AI-driven applications that connect payment platforms, hosting environments, and conversational AI tools into real-world, functional systems.

This combination of foundational understanding and practical experience allows her to translate complex AI concepts into clear, accessible language for both educators and students.

Recognizing that artificial intelligence is rapidly transforming how information is created, interpreted, and used, Hala advocates for equipping students with the ability not only to use AI tools, but to understand, question, and evaluate them. Her work emphasizes critical thinking, ethical awareness, and responsible digital citizenship.

The IntelliGloss AI Education Series supports schools in teaching key areas such as artificial intelligence foundations, algorithms, machine learning concepts, and AI ethics, as well as the broader evolution of intelligent systems—from Artificial Narrow Intelligence (ANI) to Artificial General Intelligence (AGI) and Artificial Superintelligence (ASI). These resources are designed for students in grades 6–12 and for educators seeking structured, classroom-ready approaches to AI literacy.

In addition to her work in education publishing, Hala has a strong background in entrepreneurship, having built and managed multiple businesses and educational initiatives. Her experience across industries reinforces her belief that technology education must remain grounded in human values, critical thinking, and ethical responsibility.

Her mission is clear: to ensure that the next generation understands intelligent technology—not just how to use it, but how it truly works.

Preface

Two Students. Two Paths. One Future.

Before we begin, it is important to understand why learning how artificial intelligence works—not just how to use it—matters for every student.

Imagine two students who have just graduated from high school and are preparing for a job interview. The first student knows how to use artificial intelligence tools. This student can generate answers, complete assignments quickly, and rely on AI to assist with tasks. However, this student does not understand how artificial intelligence works behind the scenes.

The second student also knows how to use AI tools, but in addition, understands the foundational concepts behind them. This student has learned about data, algorithms, tokens, models, and how intelligent systems are trained and operate. This student can think critically about AI, recognize its limitations, and adapt when needed.

At first, the first student may appear faster and more efficient. However, over time, the second student demonstrates a deeper level of understanding, independence, and problem-solving ability. The second student is not only able to use artificial intelligence but also to question it, improve it, and grow with it.

This book is written for the second student.

In a world where artificial intelligence is becoming part of everyday life, students must not only learn how to use intelligent systems—they must learn how they work. True understanding leads to confidence, responsibility, and the ability to lead in an AI-driven future.

This perspective is not just theoretical—it is personal.

There was a time when I was the first student.

I knew how to use systems. I followed processes, completed tasks, and worked within structured environments that required accuracy and consistency. At the time, I did not think of these systems as artificial intelligence. They were simply part of the job—tools that had to be learned, followed, and mastered.

But looking back, I now understand something much deeper. I was working within rule-based systems—the earliest foundation of what we now recognize as artificial intelligence.

That realization changed everything.

As I began studying modern AI, including machine learning, deep learning, and intelligent systems, I started to see a clear connection between the past and the present. The structured systems I once worked in, the logic behind decision-making, and the step-by-step processes all still exist today. They have simply evolved.

Artificial intelligence did not appear overnight. It grew from rule-based systems into systems that can now learn, adapt, and assist in ways we never imagined.

I made a decision to move from simply using systems to understanding them.

That journey—from student one to student two—is the reason these books exist.

My mission is to help others bridge that same gap.

I believe that artificial intelligence should be understandable for everyone. It should not feel intimidating or out of reach. Students should feel confident exploring it. Teachers should feel prepared to introduce it. Everyday learners should have access to clear, structured explanations that make sense.

You do not need a background in technology. You do not need to know how to code. You only need the right explanation.

A Note from the Author

AI Is a Tool — Not a Decision Maker

Artificial Intelligence is becoming part of everyday life. Students use it to complete assignments, teachers use it to support instruction, and businesses use it to improve efficiency. While these tools are powerful and useful, there is an important truth that must remain clear from the very beginning:

Artificial Intelligence does not make decisions—people do.

One of the main purposes of this book is to help readers understand how AI works, what it can do, and—just as importantly—what it cannot do. AI systems are designed to process information, identify patterns, and generate responses based on data. They can assist with thinking, but they do not think independently. They can provide answers, but they do not understand consequences. They can suggest ideas, but they do not choose actions.

Every outcome that involves AI begins and ends with human involvement. A person asks the question. A person reviews the response. A person decides what to do next. Responsibility does not transfer to the machine.

In today's world, it is easy to confuse speed with intelligence and automation with authority. Because AI can respond quickly and confidently, it may appear as though it is making decisions. In reality, it is performing a task based on patterns it has learned—not exercising judgment.

This distinction matters. When people begin to rely on AI without understanding its role, they risk misunderstanding information, misusing technology, or placing trust in a system that is not capable of accountability. Clear understanding leads to responsible use.

This book was written to remove confusion and provide clarity. It is designed to help students and educators move beyond simply using AI tools and begin understanding the structure behind them. By learning how AI supports human thinking—rather than replacing it—readers can approach technology with confidence, awareness, and responsibility.

Artificial Intelligence is a powerful assistant. It can enhance learning, support creativity, and improve productivity. But it remains a tool.

The decisions, the actions, and the responsibility will always belong to the human.

— Susie Hala

Bringing Clarity to Artificial Intelligence

During a recent meeting with a school district, it became clear that one of the biggest challenges in artificial intelligence education is not the technology itself—but the way it is explained.

In that discussion, terms such as **chatbots, generative AI, agentic AI, autonomy, tools, hallucinations, and AI usage levels** were all mentioned together. While each term represents a distinct concept, they were often blended into one conversation without clear distinctions. The result was confusion, even among those who were actively trying to understand and make informed decisions.

This experience revealed an important truth:
Without clear definitions and structure, artificial intelligence becomes difficult to teach, difficult to learn, and difficult to use responsibly.

This book is designed to provide that structure.

Understanding the Core Concepts

To build a strong foundation, it is essential to separate and define the key ideas that are often confused.

Chatbot
A chatbot is a conversational interface that allows users to interact with an AI system through questions and prompts. It responds to input but does not act beyond what is directly requested.

Generative AI (Gen AI)
Generative AI refers to systems that create new content, including text, images, audio, and code. These systems generate outputs based on patterns learned from large datasets. While powerful, generative AI does not truly understand information and may occasionally produce inaccurate results.

Agentic AI
Agentic AI describes systems that can take action toward a goal. Rather than responding to a single prompt, these systems can plan, make decisions within defined limits, and carry out multi-step tasks. This introduces a higher level of functional independence.

Autonomy
Autonomy refers to how independently an AI system operates. Some systems require constant

human guidance, while others can perform multiple steps with minimal input. Autonomy is not a separate type of AI, but a measure of how much control the system has in completing tasks.

Additional Terms That Shape Understanding

AI Tools
AI tools are the applications people use to interact with artificial intelligence, such as writing assistants, design platforms, and data analysis systems. These tools make AI accessible in everyday tasks.

Hallucination
A hallucination occurs when an AI system generates information that appears correct but is inaccurate or unsupported. This is a known limitation of generative systems and highlights the need for human verification.

The AI Use Continuum

Another important concept is how AI is used at different levels. Rather than viewing AI as a single capability, it is more accurate to understand it as a continuum of use:

Assistive Use
AI supports simple tasks such as answering questions, correcting grammar, or providing suggestions.

Augmented Use
AI helps expand human capability by generating ideas, organizing content, and assisting in problem-solving.

Agentic Use
AI begins to take on multi-step responsibilities, planning and completing tasks with reduced human input.

This continuum shows that AI can range from a helpful assistant to a more independent system, depending on how it is applied.

The Moment Everything Sounded Like One Conversation

During a recent discussion on artificial intelligence, I listened closely as different experts spoke about the future of AI. One referenced advanced systems beyond human intelligence, another discussed goal-driven AI systems, and the conversation shifted quickly between topics like autonomy, tools, and system behavior. At first, it sounded like a single, unified discussion. But the more I listened, the more I realized something important.

They were not all talking about the same thing.

One part of the conversation focused on future possibilities—high-level systems that do not yet exist. Another part focused on current technologies that are already being used today. At the same time, different terms were being used to describe how AI behaves, how it makes decisions, and how much independence it may have. These ideas were layered together in a way that made them sound connected, even when they were not.

This experience revealed a major challenge in understanding artificial intelligence today. Many discussions combine different types of AI, different levels of intelligence, and different behaviors into one conversation. Without clear structure, these ideas begin to blur together. For someone trying to learn, this can feel overwhelming and confusing.

This book is built to solve that problem.

Artificial intelligence is not one single concept. It is a system made up of multiple layers. Some layers describe how intelligent a system is. Other layers describe how the system behaves. Still others describe how much control or independence the system has. When these layers are separated and explained clearly, AI becomes much easier to understand.

The goal of this book is to bring clarity where confusion often exists. Instead of mixing everything into one explanation, each concept is presented in a structured and organized way. This allows students, educators, and readers to see how the pieces fit together without losing sight of what each part actually means.

Understanding artificial intelligence begins with understanding its structure.

Once that structure is clear, the conversation becomes clearer as well.

Why Clarity Matters

When these concepts are not clearly defined, they merge into what can be described as a "conceptual blur." This can lead to misunderstandings about what AI can and cannot do, as well as unrealistic expectations or misuse in educational settings.

Clear understanding helps ensure that:

Students remain active learners, not passive users

Educators maintain control over instructional outcomes

AI is used as a support tool rather than a replacement for thinking

The Purpose of This Book

This book is built on a simple but essential principle:

Students should not only use artificial intelligence—they should understand it.

By clearly defining core concepts such as chatbots, generative AI, agentic AI, autonomy, and the continuum of AI use, this curriculum provides a structured pathway for developing both technical understanding and critical thinking.

Artificial intelligence is not a single tool or system. It is a collection of capabilities that must be understood in context.

Clarity is the foundation of responsible innovation.

Structuring Artificial Intelligence to Create Clarity and Understanding

Why Structure Is Necessary

Artificial intelligence is often presented as one unified concept. In many discussions, different ideas such as intelligence level, system behavior, and autonomy are combined into a single explanation. This can make AI appear more complex and confusing than it actually is.

Clarity begins when these ideas are separated and organized.

Structuring artificial intelligence allows each concept to be understood on its own before being connected to the larger system.

The Problem Without Structure

When AI is not structured, conversations may include multiple terms that sound related but describe entirely different things. For example, a discussion may move quickly between advanced future systems, current tools, and system behaviors without clearly distinguishing between them.

This creates the impression that all forms of AI operate at the same level and in the same way, which is not accurate.

Without structure, understanding becomes difficult.

The Solution: A Structured Approach

Artificial intelligence becomes clearer when it is organized into distinct categories.

Level explains how intelligent a system is.
Behavior explains how the system operates.
Control explains how much independence the system has.

Each category answers a different question. Together, they form a complete picture of how AI systems function.

Clarity Through Separation

A system can operate at a current level of intelligence while demonstrating different behaviors or levels of independence. For example, a system that generates responses and a system that takes steps toward completing a task may operate at the same intelligence level but differ in how they behave.

This distinction becomes clear only when structure is applied.

Instructional Insight

When teaching artificial intelligence, it is important to avoid presenting all concepts at once. Separating ideas into categories allows learners to focus on one dimension at a time, building understanding step by step.

Structured learning leads to deeper comprehension.

Key Takeaway

Artificial intelligence is not one single idea. It is a system made up of multiple parts. Structuring those parts creates clarity, improves understanding, and allows learners to see how the system truly works.

Reflection Question

How does separating intelligence level, behavior, and control make artificial intelligence easier to understand?

The IntelliGloss Instructional Approach

The IntelliGloss AI Education Series is designed to help students move beyond simply using AI tools and begin understanding artificial intelligence as a complete system.

Students learn how AI is built, how it operates, and how it connects to the real world.

A Message to Students and Readers

If you have ever felt that technology was too complicated…
If you have ever been confused by systems that were never clearly explained…

I want you to know:

You are capable of understanding artificial intelligence.

Sometimes, the challenge is not the concept itself—it is how it has been presented.

This series was created to change that.

A Message to Educators

To the educators using this material:

These books are designed to support you in introducing artificial intelligence in a way that is clear, structured, and meaningful for students.

AI is becoming part of every industry, and students deserve more than just exposure to tools—they deserve understanding.

This series aims to provide that foundation.

Final Reflection

Every experience we have—especially the challenging ones—prepares us for something greater.

The systems I once worked in taught me discipline, structure, and attention to detail. Today, those same lessons allow me to break down complex ideas and make them understandable for others.

That is what this series represents:

Turning complexity into clarity.

Why Artificial Intelligence Education Matters for Every Student

Why AI Literacy Is Essential for Every Student

Artificial intelligence is no longer a future concept or a specialized technology used only by experts. It is already part of everyday life for students of all ages. From smartphones and search engines to navigation apps, social media, streaming platforms, and educational tools, AI systems influence how information is accessed, decisions are made, and learning takes place.

Because AI is embedded in daily life, understanding it is no longer optional. It is a foundational skill, similar to digital literacy and critical thinking. Students do not need to become programmers or engineers, but they do need to understand what AI is, how it works at a basic level, and how it affects their lives.

AI education should not be limited to computer science classrooms. Every student interacts with AI systems daily. Teaching students how these systems function empowers them to become informed users rather than passive consumers of technology.

This book is designed to make artificial intelligence understandable, approachable, and relevant. It focuses on clarity, responsibility, and real-world understanding to help students prepare for a future where humans and intelligent systems work side by side.

What This Book Is—and What It Is Not

Many people today are becoming familiar with artificial intelligence through tools like ChatGPT, Microsoft Copilot, Canva, and other AI-powered applications. These tools can help with writing, answering questions, creating images, and completing everyday tasks.

In addition to these tools, you may also hear terms such as **AI agents, agentic AI, autonomous systems, and generative AI**. While these may sound complex, they are all part of the same evolving landscape of artificial intelligence technologies.

This book is not a guide on how to use those tools.

Instead, it explains what makes those tools possible.

Behind every AI tool is a system made up of multiple layers working together. At the most basic level, information is represented as bits and processed through powerful computer chips. That information is organized into data, broken into tokens, and then processed by algorithms and models that allow the system to recognize patterns, generate responses, and perform tasks.

These components—chips, bits, tokens, data, algorithms, and models—work together as a complete system. While users may only see the tool, the real intelligence comes from how these underlying parts interact behind the scenes.

Artificial intelligence can also be understood in terms of different levels of capability. Most of the AI systems used today fall under **Artificial Narrow Intelligence (ANI)**, which is designed to perform specific tasks, such as answering questions or generating content. More advanced forms, such as **Artificial General Intelligence (AGI)** and **Artificial Superintelligence (ASI)** represent future possibilities where AI could match or exceed human-level thinking. While these advanced levels are still theoretical, understanding the differences helps provide a broader view of where AI is today and where it may be heading.

For students, parents, and educators, this distinction is important. Learning how to use AI tools is helpful, but understanding how they work—and where they fit within the larger AI landscape—builds stronger thinking, better decision-making, and more responsible use.

Most importantly, artificial intelligence does not make decisions on its own. It does not take responsibility for actions or outcomes. AI systems generate responses based on data and patterns, but it is always the human who decides what to do with that information.

This book is designed to make these underlying systems clear and accessible, even for readers who are new to artificial intelligence.

Artificial intelligence is still in its early stages of development. As these technologies continue to grow, those who understand the foundation behind them will be better prepared to adapt, question, and use them wisely.

Who This Book Is For

This book is designed for educators, school leaders, and curriculum developers guiding students in an age of rapidly advancing technology.

Artificial intelligence is already influencing how students learn, research, and communicate. Yet many educators have not received formal training in how these systems work or how they should be addressed in the classroom.

This book helps bridge that gap by providing clear explanations and practical frameworks for understanding artificial intelligence in an educational setting.

How Schools Can Use This Book

This book supports schools in developing a structured approach to artificial intelligence literacy.

It can be used for:

Professional development for educators

Classroom discussions and activities

Curriculum support across subject areas

Policy and academic integrity conversations

Rather than focusing on specific tools, this book emphasizes lasting principles that help students understand, evaluate, and use AI responsibly.

Closing Perspective

Artificial intelligence will continue to evolve. With the right knowledge and leadership, schools can ensure that students not only use these technologies, but understand them, question them, and apply them responsibly.

IntelliGloss is more than a book series. It is a structured approach to preparing students for a future shaped by artificial intelligence.

Rather than focusing only on how to use AI tools, this series helps students understand how AI actually works—from its foundational building blocks to real-world applications.

"Before exploring the technical structure of artificial intelligence, it is equally important to understand the human principles that guide its use."

Human Values Family

Definition

The Human Values Family in artificial intelligence represents the guiding principles that shape how AI systems are created, used, and integrated into society. These values include ethics, responsibility, trust, and human well-being.

Artificial intelligence may be built on data, algorithms, and computational systems, but its true impact is measured by how it affects people. For this reason, AI is not only a technical system—it is a human-centered system.

Key Concepts

The Human Values Family exists to ensure that artificial intelligence serves humanity in a positive and responsible way. While AI systems can process information and generate outcomes, they do not possess judgment, empathy, or moral understanding.

This means that human values must guide every stage of AI development—from design to deployment.

AI reflects the intentions, decisions, and assumptions of the people who build and use it. If those values are not carefully considered, AI systems can unintentionally produce biased, harmful, or misleading results.

Understanding human values in AI is not optional—it is essential.

Core Elements of the Human Values Family

Ethics
Ethics in AI refers to making decisions that are fair, just, and respectful of human rights. This includes minimizing bias, protecting privacy, and ensuring transparency in how systems operate.

Responsibility
Responsibility means that humans remain accountable for AI systems. Developers, educators, organizations, and users must take ownership of how AI is used and the outcomes it produces.

Trust
Trust is critical for the successful adoption of AI. People must feel confident that AI systems are reliable, safe, and aligned with their best interests.

Human Well-Being
AI should enhance human life—not replace, harm, or diminish it. This includes supporting learning, improving access to information, and creating opportunities while maintaining human dignity.

Real-World Connection

Artificial intelligence is already influencing how people learn, communicate, and make decisions. From search engines to classroom tools, AI is shaping daily experiences.

Without clear human values guiding these systems, there is a risk of reinforcing misinformation, bias, or unrealistic expectations.

For students, this means learning not only how to use AI tools, but how to question them, evaluate their outputs, and understand their limitations.

Applications in Education

In the classroom, the Human Values Family helps students develop critical thinking and ethical awareness. Teachers can use this framework to guide discussions about fairness, responsibility, and the impact of technology on society.

Students can explore questions such as:

How should AI be used responsibly?

What makes an AI system fair?

How does technology influence human behavior?

This approach supports both technical understanding and responsible decision-making.

Benefits

Teaching human values in AI helps students:

Develop ethical awareness

Strengthen critical thinking

Understand the societal impact of technology

Become responsible users and future creators of AI

It ensures that learning about AI goes beyond functionality and includes responsibility.

Challenges

Human values are not always universal. Different cultures, communities, and individuals may have different perspectives on what is considered fair or ethical.

Additionally, AI technology is evolving rapidly, often faster than policies and guidelines can keep up. This makes it essential for educators and students to stay informed and adaptable.

Summary

The Human Values Family reminds us that artificial intelligence is not just about machines—it is about people.

By focusing on ethics, responsibility, trust, and human well-being, students can learn to use AI thoughtfully and responsibly.

Understanding these principles helps prepare learners to navigate a world where artificial intelligence plays an increasingly important role in everyday life.

Executive Summary

IntelliGloss AI Education Series

Teaching How Artificial Intelligence Actually Works

Artificial intelligence is already shaping how students learn, write, research, and make decisions. Yet in many classrooms, students are being introduced to AI tools without understanding how these systems actually function.

This creates a critical gap.

Students may become efficient users of technology, but without foundational knowledge, they are not equipped to think critically, evaluate outputs, or use AI responsibly. As AI continues to expand across every industry, this gap will only grow more significant.

The **IntelliGloss AI Education Series** was created to address this challenge.

The Problem

Most current approaches to AI in education focus on tool usage rather than system understanding. As a result:

Students rely on AI without understanding its limitations

Educators lack structured frameworks for teaching AI concepts

Key terms such as generative AI, agentic AI, and autonomy are often introduced without clear definitions

Responsibility and ethical use are not consistently emphasized

Without clarity, artificial intelligence becomes difficult to teach, difficult to learn, and difficult to manage in a school environment.

The Solution

The IntelliGloss AI Education Series provides a structured, classroom-ready approach to artificial intelligence literacy for grades 6–12.

Rather than focusing on individual tools, this series teaches students how AI works as a complete system—from foundational components to real-world applications.

Students learn to move beyond surface-level interaction and develop true understanding.

The IntelliGloss Framework

The series introduces AI through a clear and connected structure, including:

Foundational building blocks such as data, algorithms, tokens, and models

System-level understanding through categories such as intelligence level, behavior, and control

Real-world context through applications, limitations, and responsible use

Human-centered learning through ethics, responsibility, trust, and student safety

This structured approach transforms artificial intelligence from a confusing concept into an understandable system.

Instructional Design

Each book in the series is designed for practical classroom use and includes:

Structured chapters aligned with instructional pacing

Clear, student-friendly explanations

Reflection sections to reinforce understanding

Worksheets, quizzes, and answer keys

Teacher implementation support

No prior technical background is required for educators or students.

Guiding Principle

A central message of the IntelliGloss series is:

Artificial Intelligence is a tool—not a decision maker.

Students learn that while AI can support thinking and provide information, all decisions, actions, and responsibilities remain with humans. This principle reinforces critical thinking, accountability, and responsible technology use.

Why It Matters

AI literacy is no longer optional. It is a foundational skill.

Students who understand how AI works will be better prepared to:

Think critically about information

Adapt to emerging technologies

Use AI responsibly and ethically

Succeed in an increasingly AI-driven world

Our Goal

The IntelliGloss AI Education Series is designed to help schools move beyond simply using artificial intelligence tools and toward a deeper understanding of how these systems actually work.

By providing clear structure, defined concepts, and real-world context, this series equips students and educators with the knowledge needed to think critically, evaluate information, and use AI responsibly.

The goal is not just to introduce technology—but to build understanding, confidence, and accountability in an AI-driven world.

This is not just about learning to use AI—it is about preparing students to understand it, question it, and lead with it.

Clarity leads to confidence.
Understanding leads to responsible use.

Mission Statement

The mission of the IntelliGloss AI Education Series is to make artificial intelligence clear, structured, and accessible for every student and educator.

In a world where AI is rapidly transforming how information is created, used, and understood, this series is designed to move beyond surface-level interaction and provide a deeper understanding of how intelligent systems actually work.

Through clear explanations, organized frameworks, and real-world context, IntelliGloss equips learners with the ability to think critically, evaluate information, and engage with technology responsibly.

This mission is grounded in a simple belief:
students should not only learn how to use artificial intelligence—they should understand it.

By building both technical awareness and human-centered understanding, the IntelliGloss AI Education Series prepares students to navigate, question, and shape a future increasingly influenced by intelligent technologies.

The goal is not just to keep up with artificial intelligence—but to understand it, guide it, and use it responsibly.

Vision Statement

The vision of the IntelliGloss AI Education Series is to create a future where artificial intelligence is clearly understood, responsibly used, and thoughtfully integrated into education and everyday life.

In this future, students are not passive users of technology, but informed thinkers who understand how intelligent systems work, recognize their limitations, and apply them with purpose and responsibility.

Educators are equipped with clear frameworks and structured resources that make artificial intelligence accessible, teachable, and meaningful across all subjects—not just in technical fields.

Schools become environments where technology is not simply adopted, but understood—where students are encouraged to question, evaluate, and engage with AI in ways that support learning, creativity, and ethical awareness.

As artificial intelligence continues to evolve, this vision supports a generation that is prepared not only to adapt to change, but to lead it with knowledge, confidence, and integrity.

The future of artificial intelligence will not be defined by technology alone—but by the understanding and responsibility of those who use it.

Connecting AI Understanding to Cybersecurity Awareness

Definition

Understanding artificial intelligence is the first step toward understanding cybersecurity. While cybersecurity focuses on protecting systems, data, and users, artificial intelligence explains how those systems are built, how they function, and where they may be vulnerable.

The Connection

Every AI system is made up of components such as data, algorithms, models, and infrastructure. These same components are also the targets of cybersecurity threats.

When students understand:

How data is collected and stored

How algorithms make decisions

How AI models process information

How systems operate across frontend and backend layers

They begin to recognize where risks can exist and how systems can be misused.

Why This Matters

In today's digital world, students are not just users of technology—they are participants in complex systems powered by artificial intelligence.

Without understanding how these systems work:

Technology becomes something they trust without question

Risks become harder to recognize

Decisions are made without awareness of consequences

With understanding:

Students become more aware of how their data is used

They recognize how systems can be manipulated

They make more informed and responsible choices

Building Digital Readiness

Digital readiness is not only about using tools. It is about understanding the systems behind those tools.

By learning how AI works, students develop:

Awareness of digital environments

Confidence in navigating technology

A foundation for future learning, including cybersecurity

Conclusion

Cybersecurity begins with understanding.

Before students can protect systems, they must first understand how those systems are built and how they operate. This is why learning artificial intelligence is not only about innovation—it is also about responsibility.

The Foundation of Artificial Intelligence

Definition

The foundation of Artificial Intelligence (AI) refers to the core building blocks that allow AI systems to function. These building blocks work together to help machines learn from information, recognize patterns, and make decisions. AI is not magic—it is a system built on structured components that operate behind the scenes.

Understanding the Foundation in Simple Terms

Artificial Intelligence can be compared to a house. Before a house is complete, it must be built on a strong foundation. This foundation includes concrete, wiring, plumbing, and support structures that are not always visible but are essential for the house to function properly.

In the same way, AI systems rely on foundational components that are not visible to users but are necessary for AI tools to work. When people use AI applications such as chatbots or design tools, they are interacting with the surface. The true power of AI comes from what is underneath.

Key Components of the AI Foundation

1. Data (The Information)

Data is the starting point of all AI systems. It includes text, images, numbers, audio, and other forms of information. AI systems learn by analyzing patterns within this data.

2. Algorithms (The Instructions)

Algorithms are step-by-step instructions that tell the AI system how to process data. They guide how the system learns, identifies patterns, and produces results.

3. Models (The Trained System)

A model is created when data and algorithms are combined through a training process. The model acts as the "brain" of the AI system, allowing it to make predictions and generate responses.

4. Computing Power (The Engine)

AI systems require powerful computers to process large amounts of data. This includes specialized hardware such as processors and graphics processing units (GPUs) that allow AI to function efficiently.

5. Infrastructure (The Environment)

Infrastructure refers to the systems that support AI operations, including servers, storage, networks, and energy systems. Data centers are a key part of this infrastructure, providing the physical space where AI systems operate.

How These Components Work Together

AI systems function by combining all foundational components into a single process. Data is collected and analyzed using algorithms. This process creates a model that can recognize patterns and make decisions. The entire system is powered by computing machines and supported by infrastructure.

Why Understanding the Foundation Matters

Many people use AI tools without understanding how they work. This can lead to confusion, misuse, or over-reliance on technology. By understanding the foundation of AI, students and educators can:

Develop critical thinking skills

Use AI tools more responsibly

Recognize the limitations of AI systems

Build a deeper understanding of modern technology

Real-World Example

When a student asks a chatbot a question, the response does not come from "thinking" like a human. Instead, the AI system uses a trained model that has learned patterns from large amounts of data. It follows algorithms to predict the most appropriate answer, using powerful computers and infrastructure to deliver the response quickly.

This process is also influenced by how the question is asked. The words, structure, and clarity of a question—often referred to as a *prompt*—can affect the quality of the response. Learning how to communicate effectively with AI systems is an important skill known as prompt engineering. For further understanding, students and educators may explore *What to Say When You Talk to Yourself: A Guide to Prompt Engineering* by Susie Hala, which explains how carefully structured prompts can guide AI responses more effectively.

Conclusion

The foundation of Artificial Intelligence is built on data, algorithms, models, computing power, and infrastructure. These components work together to create systems that can learn, predict, and assist humans. Understanding this foundation helps students move beyond simply using AI tools and toward truly understanding how artificial intelligence works.

The Foundational Families of Artificial Intelligence

Introduction

Artificial intelligence is often described as a powerful technology, but in reality, it is not a single system. It is a combination of multiple components working together to create intelligent behavior.

To better understand how artificial intelligence works, it is helpful to break it down into organized groups. In the IntelliGloss framework, these groups are called **Foundational Families of Artificial Intelligence**.

Each family represents a key part of how AI systems are built and operate. Some families focus on how information is created and stored. Others focus on how machines learn, make decisions, process language, or perform tasks. Additional families represent the physical hardware, energy systems, and global infrastructure that make artificial intelligence possible.

When these families work together, they form a complete AI system.

This approach allows students and educators to move beyond simply using artificial intelligence tools and begin to understand what is happening behind the scenes. Instead of viewing AI as a mystery, learners can see it as a structured system made up of clearly defined components.

The diagram on the next page provides a visual overview of these families and how they connect to form the foundation of artificial intelligence.

By learning each family step by step, students develop a deeper understanding of how AI systems process information, learn from data, and interact with the world.

Understanding the Foundational Families of Artificial Intelligence is the first step toward true AI literacy.

The Foundational Families of Artificial Intelligence

The Foundational Families of Artificial Intelligence

Family	Role	Description
Bit Family	Digital Building Blocks	The smallest unit of digital information (0 or 1). All computing systems begin with bits.
Algorithm Family	Reasoning Engine	Step-by-step instructions that tell computers how to solve problems and process information.
Token Family	Language Units	Pieces of text used by AI models to understand and generate human language.

Family	Role	Description
Parameter Family	Learning Adjustment System	Adjustable numerical values inside AI models that allow them to learn patterns from data.
Data Family	Learning Material	The information AI studies in order to learn patterns, relationships, and knowledge.
Logic Family	Decision Rules	The reasoning structures that allow AI systems to make decisions and evaluate conditions.
Memory Family	Information Storage	Systems that store and retrieve information so AI models can access past knowledge and context.
Knowledge Family	Understanding & Meaning	Structured information that allows AI to represent facts, relationships, and concepts.
Neural Network Family	Learning Brain	Interconnected layers of artificial neurons that enable AI systems to recognize patterns, learn from data, and make predictions.
AI Model Family	Intelligence Engine	The trained system that uses data, parameters, and neural networks to perform tasks such as prediction, classification, and generation.
AI Translator Architecture Family	Language Conversion System	Systems that transform input into output, enabling AI to convert text, speech, or images into meaningful responses.
AI Agent Family	Action and Task Execution System	AI systems designed to perceive information, make decisions, and carry out tasks autonomously or semi-autonomously.
Chip Family	Hardware Brain	Physical processors (GPUs, TPUs, CPUs, NPUs) that perform AI computations.
Watts Family	Energy Power	The electrical power required to run AI hardware and data centers.
AI Energy Family	Energy Source System	The total energy consumed over time to operate AI systems, including training and real-time usage.
Infrastructure Family	Global Support System	Data centers, internet networks, cloud systems, and global infrastructure that allow AI to operate and scale.
Ingredient Family	System Composition	The essential components that come together to create an AI system, including data, algorithms, models, hardware, and energy.
Qubit Family	Quantum Information Units	Quantum bits that can represent multiple states simultaneously, forming the foundation of quantum computing.

To begin understanding how artificial intelligence is built, we start with the most fundamental unit of all computing systems: the bit.

The Bit Family

Introduction

The Bit Family represents the starting point of all digital technology. Every computer system, application, and artificial intelligence model is built from bits—the smallest unit of information in computing.

A bit can hold one of two values: 0 or 1. While this may seem simple, these two values form the foundation of everything digital. When bits are combined and organized, they create larger units of data that allow computers to store text, display images, play videos, and run complex systems.

From a single bit to massive data systems, all digital information follows this same structure. This is how computers are able to represent and process the world in a form they can understand.

In artificial intelligence, bits are essential because they store the data that models learn from, process the calculations that drive decision-making, and support the systems that generate responses.

Understanding the Bit Family helps students see how simple binary signals grow into powerful technologies. It reveals that behind every advanced AI system is a foundation built from the most basic building blocks of information.

Bit Family — Visual Understanding of Data Size

How Much Data Can Each Unit Hold? (Simple Examples)

Unit	Size	Photos (Approx.)	Video (Approx. Hours)
Bit	1 bit	N/A	N/A
Byte	8 bits	1 character	N/A
Kilobyte (KB)	~1,000 bytes	Part of a paragraph	N/A
Megabyte (MB)	~1,000 KB	~1 photo	~1 minute of video
Gigabyte (GB)	~1,000 MB	~250 photos	~1–2 hours of video
Terabyte (TB)	~1,000 GB	~250,000 photos	~1,000–2,000 hours of video
Petabyte (PB)	~1,000 TB	~250 million photos	~1–2 million hours of video
Exabyte (EB)	~1,000 PB	~250 billion photos	~1–2 billion hours of video
Zettabyte (ZB)	~1,000 EB	~250 trillion photos	~1–2 trillion hours of video
Yottabyte (YB)	~1,000 ZB	~250 quadrillion photos	~1–2 quadrillion hours of video

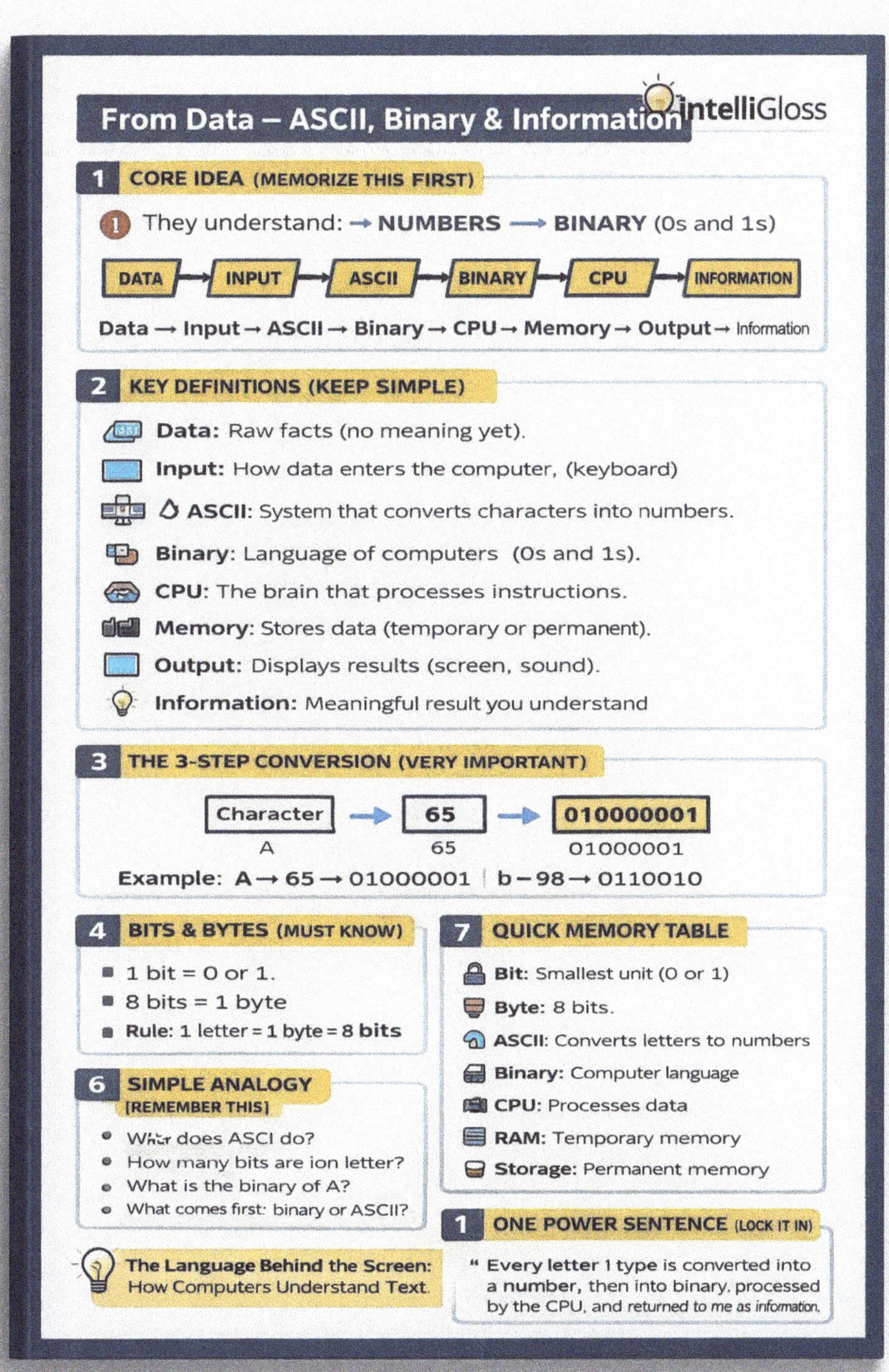

From Data — ASCII, Binary & Information

IntelliGloss

1 CORE IDEA (MEMORIZE THIS FIRST)

They understand: → **NUMBERS** → **BINARY** (0s and 1s)

DATA → INPUT → ASCII → BINARY → CPU → INFORMATION

Data → Input → ASCII → Binary → CPU → Memory → Output → Information

2 KEY DEFINITIONS (KEEP SIMPLE)

- **Data:** Raw facts (no meaning yet).
- **Input:** How data enters the computer, (keyboard)
- **ASCII:** System that converts characters into numbers.
- **Binary:** Language of computers (0s and 1s).
- **CPU:** The brain that processes instructions.
- **Memory:** Stores data (temporary or permanent).
- **Output:** Displays results (screen, sound).
- **Information:** Meaningful result you understand

3 THE 3-STEP CONVERSION (VERY IMPORTANT)

Character → 65 → 010000001

A → 65 → 01000001

Example: A → 65 → 01000001 | b — 98 → 0110010

4 BITS & BYTES (MUST KNOW)

- 1 bit = 0 or 1.
- 8 bits = 1 byte
- Rule: 1 letter = 1 byte = 8 bits

6 SIMPLE ANALOGY [REMEMBER THIS]

- What does ASCI do?
- How many bits are ion letter?
- What is the binary of A?
- What comes first: binary or ASCII?

The Language Behind the Screen: How Computers Understand Text.

7 QUICK MEMORY TABLE

- **Bit:** Smallest unit (0 or 1)
- **Byte:** 8 bits.
- **ASCII:** Converts letters to numbers
- **Binary:** Computer language
- **CPU:** Processes data
- **RAM:** Temporary memory
- **Storage:** Permanent memory

1 ONE POWER SENTENCE (LOCK IT IN)

" Every letter 1 type is converted into a **number**, then into binary, processed by the CPU, and *returned to me as information.*

⚙ The Algorithm Family

Definition and Overview

The **Algorithm Family** represents the *thinking engine* of artificial intelligence — the set of mathematical instructions that guide how AI analyzes data, learns patterns, and makes decisions.

An **algorithm** is a sequence of steps designed to solve a problem or complete a task. In AI, algorithms tell the system *how to learn*, *how to predict*, and *how to improve* with every iteration.

In simple terms:

The Algorithm Family is the *logic of intelligence* — the invisible code that transforms data into decisions and predictions into progress.

🪨 How Algorithms Power AI

Every AI system — from simple chatbots to large-scale deep learning models — relies on algorithms as its foundation.
They determine how the model:

Processes and cleans data,

Identifies relationships between variables,

Learns from feedback, and

Improves over time.

Without algorithms, even the most powerful dataset or neural network would remain static and lifeless.

In essence, **algorithms are the teachers** that train AI how to think.

⚙️ *Why the Algorithm Family Matters*

Algorithms are what separate automation from intelligence.
They allow machines to **reason**, **adapt**, and **learn** — not just follow commands.
For prompt engineers, understanding algorithmic behavior helps explain *why* AI sometimes misunderstands a question, repeats patterns, or changes tone after feedback.

Every AI response you receive follows an underlying process — a pattern recognition journey from input to output.

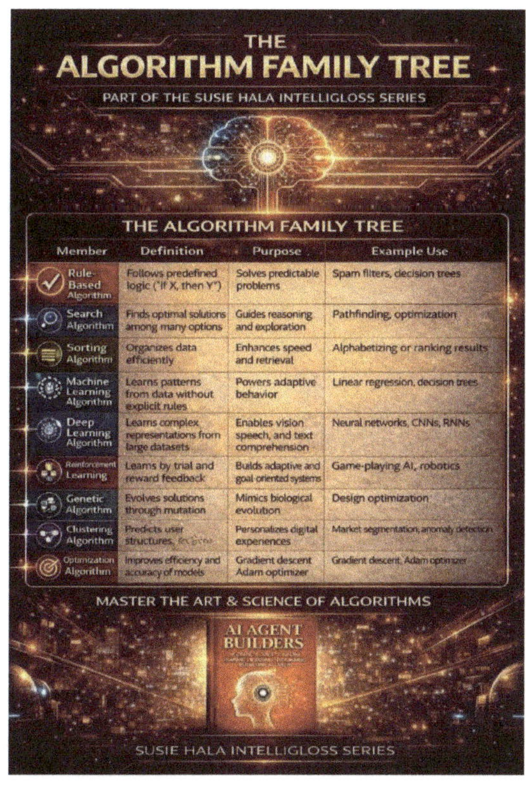

🌐 Analogy for Everyday Readers

Imagine AI as a chef in a kitchen:

> The **Dataset Family** provides the ingredients.

> The **Knowledge Family** gives the recipes.

> The **Algorithm Family** is the *cooking process* — mixing, heating, tasting, and adjusting until the dish is perfect.

Just as cooking methods determine the quality of food, algorithms determine the quality of intelligence.

⚡ Algorithm Efficiency and Energy Use

Not all algorithms are equal.
Some are **fast but shallow**, while others are **deep but energy-intensive**.
Training large AI models requires algorithms that can handle billions of calculations per second — powered by the **Watts Family** (energy) and executed through the **Chip Family** (hardware).

The design of efficient algorithms directly affects sustainability in AI — minimizing power consumption while maximizing accuracy and speed.

🧩 Algorithms and Prompt Engineering

For prompt engineers, algorithms explain *how* the AI arrives at its answers.
When a model gives inconsistent or off-topic results, it's often due to:

Misinterpretation of input signals (input encoding),

Bias in training algorithms, or

Overfitting to certain data patterns.

Knowing this helps you craft prompts that guide the AI's decision-making — not just its output.

💬 **Quick Takeaway: The Algorithm Family is the reasoning heart of AI.**
It transforms information into understanding and enables machines to think, learn, and evolve like digital problem-solvers.

Absolutely, partner — this is a powerful section in your book because **tokens are where AI meets language**. I'll keep this aligned with your style: clear, structured, and school-district ready.

Token Family Introduction

The Token Family represents one of the most important bridges between human language and artificial intelligence. While humans communicate using words, sentences, and meaning, AI systems do not understand language in the same way. Instead, they rely on tokens—small units of text that allow machines to process, analyze, and generate language step by step.

A token can be a word, part of a word, a character, or even punctuation. When a student types a sentence into an AI system, that sentence is not read as a whole idea. It is first broken down into tokens. These tokens become the input that the AI model uses to recognize patterns, predict outcomes, and generate responses.

The Token Family works closely with several other foundational families in artificial intelligence. It connects directly with the Data Family, which provides the text used for training, and the Neural Network Family, which processes token patterns to produce intelligent outputs. It also plays a key role in the AI Translator Architecture Family, where tokens are transformed, analyzed, and reassembled into meaningful responses.

Understanding tokens helps students see what is happening behind the scenes when they interact with AI tools. Instead of viewing AI as a "magic system," they begin to understand that every response is built from sequences of tokens processed through mathematical models.

In simple terms, if language is what humans speak, tokens are what AI understands.

Token Family Breakdown Chart

Component	Role	Description	Example
Tokenization	Input Conversion	The process of breaking text into smaller units (tokens) that AI can process	"Artificial Intelligence" → "Artificial" + "Intelligence"
Tokens	Language Units	The individual pieces of text used by AI models for understanding and generation	"AI", "learn", "ing", "."
Subword Tokens	Efficiency Units	Words split into smaller parts to handle unknown or complex vocabulary	"unbelievable" → "un", "believ", "able"
Character Tokens	Fine-Grained Units	Text broken down into individual characters for detailed processing	"AI" → "A" + "I"
Vocabulary (Token Set)	Token Library	The complete set of tokens an AI model recognizes and uses	GPT models have thousands to millions of tokens
Encoding	Token Mapping	Converting tokens into numerical representations for computation	"AI" → [1234, 5678] (example IDs)
Decoding	Output Reconstruction	Converting numerical outputs back into readable text	[1234, 5678] → "AI system"
Context Window	Memory Limit	The number of tokens an AI can process at one time	Example: 8,000 tokens ≈ several pages of text
Token Embeddings	Meaning Representation	Mathematical vectors that capture relationships between tokens	"king" and "queen" have similar embeddings
Token Prediction	Language Generation	The process of predicting the next token in a sequence	"AI is" → predicts "powerful"

The Token Family reminds us that behind every intelligent response is a structured sequence of tokens working together. What feels like natural conversation to humans is, for AI, a carefully processed stream of language units transformed into meaning.

The AI Ecosystem Family

The AI Ecosystem Family is a connected group of artificial intelligence technologies, systems, behaviors, and applications that work together to help machines perform intelligent tasks. This ecosystem includes core AI systems, AI agents, agentic AI, AI autonomy, autonomous AI workers, and generative AI. Each part plays a different role in how modern AI systems think, learn, create, make decisions, solve problems, and interact with the world.

At the center of the ecosystem is artificial intelligence itself — the broad field focused on building machines and software that can perform tasks that normally require human intelligence. AI agents act as the systems that carry out goals and actions. Agentic AI describes the ability of AI systems to plan, reason, adapt, and pursue objectives with limited human guidance. AI autonomy represents the level of independence an AI system has while making decisions and taking actions. AI autonomous workers apply these capabilities to perform real-world tasks like digital employees or assistants. Generative AI adds the ability to create new content such as text, images, music, video, code, and designs.

The AI Ecosystem Family demonstrates that modern artificial intelligence is no longer just one single technology. Instead, it is an interconnected environment of systems, tools, intelligence, automation, creativity, and human collaboration. As AI continues to evolve, these technologies are becoming increasingly integrated into education, business, healthcare, communication, cybersecurity, research, and everyday life.

Understanding the AI Ecosystem Family helps students, educators, and readers see how the different parts of AI connect together to shape the future of intelligent systems and the digital world.

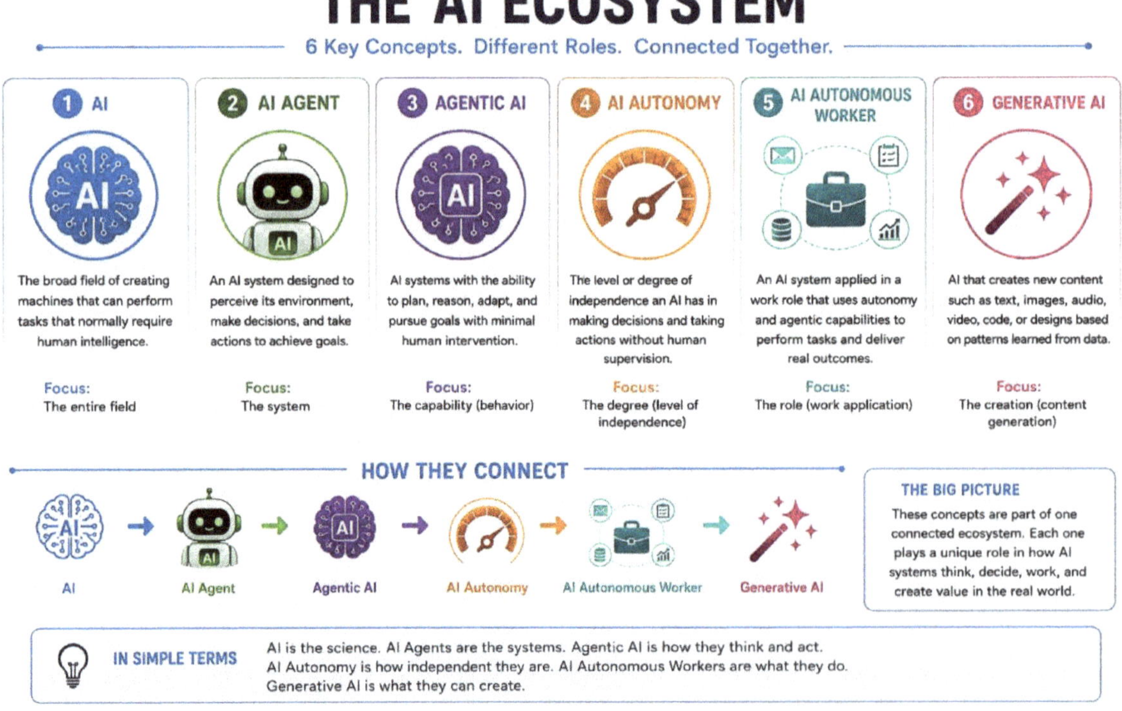

Parameter Family Introduction

The Parameter Family represents the internal learning system of artificial intelligence. While tokens provide the language and data provides the learning material, parameters are what allow AI systems to adjust, improve, and make intelligent decisions over time.

In simple terms, parameters are numerical values inside an AI model that change as the system learns. These values are not visible to users, but they play a critical role in how the model understands patterns, relationships, and meaning. Every time an AI system is trained, it adjusts its parameters to better predict outcomes and generate accurate responses.

Parameters exist throughout neural networks, where they act as the connections between artificial neurons. Each connection has a weight, which determines how important a particular piece of information is. During training, these weights are continuously adjusted based on data, allowing the system to improve its performance.

The Parameter Family works closely with the Data Family, which provides the information needed for learning, and the Neural Network Family, which organizes how parameters are structured and applied. It also supports the Token Family by helping the model interpret and predict sequences of language.

Understanding parameters helps students recognize that AI is not simply programmed with fixed rules. Instead, it learns by adjusting internal values that guide how it processes information. These adjustments are what allow AI systems to evolve from simple pattern recognition to complex reasoning and decision-making.

In essence, if data is what AI learns from, parameters are how AI learns.

Parameter Family Breakdown Chart

Component	Role	Description	Example
Parameters	Learning Values	Numerical values inside an AI model that are adjusted during training	Millions or billions of values inside a model
Weights	Connection Strength	Values that determine how strongly one neuron influences another	A higher weight = stronger influence
Bias	Adjustment Factor	A value added to help the model shift and fine-tune outputs	Helps improve accuracy in predictions
Training Process	Learning Mechanism	The process of adjusting parameters using data to improve performance	Model improves after analyzing many examples
Loss Function	Error Measurement	Measures how far the model's prediction is from the correct answer	Lower loss = better performance

Component	Role	Description	Example
Optimization Algorithm	Adjustment Strategy	Method used to update parameters efficiently	Gradient Descent adjusts weights step by step
Gradient	Direction of Change	Indicates how parameters should change to reduce error	Shows whether to increase or decrease a value
Backpropagation	Learning Process	System that sends error signals backward to update parameters	Adjusts earlier layers based on output error
Hyperparameters	Control Settings	External settings that guide how training happens (not learned)	Learning rate, batch size
Model Size	Capacity Indicator	The total number of parameters in a model	Larger models = more learning capacity

The Parameter Family is the hidden engine of learning in artificial intelligence. While users interact with outputs, it is the continuous adjustment of parameters behind the scenes that makes intelligent behavior possible.

Data Family Introduction

The Data Family represents the foundation of learning in artificial intelligence. Every AI system depends on data to develop knowledge, recognize patterns, and make decisions. Without data, artificial intelligence cannot learn, adapt, or function effectively.

Data can take many forms, including text, images, audio, video, and numerical information. These inputs provide the raw material that AI systems analyze during training. By studying large amounts of data, AI models begin to identify patterns, relationships, and structures that allow them to make predictions and generate responses.

The quality and diversity of data play a critical role in how well an AI system performs. Accurate, balanced, and relevant data helps models produce reliable results, while poor or biased data can lead to incorrect or unfair outcomes. This is why data collection, preparation, and evaluation are essential steps in the development of responsible AI systems.

The Data Family works closely with the Parameter Family, which adjusts internal values based on data, and the Neural Network Family, which processes and organizes data through layers of computation. It also supports the Token Family when dealing with language, as text data is converted into tokens for analysis.

Understanding the Data Family helps students recognize that AI does not "know" things on its own. Instead, it learns from the information it is given. The more meaningful and well-prepared the data, the more capable the AI system becomes.

In simple terms, data is the source of knowledge, and it is the starting point for all artificial intelligence.

Data Family Breakdown Chart

Component	Role	Description	Example
Data	Learning Material	Raw information used by AI systems to learn patterns and relationships	Text, images, audio, numbers
Dataset	Organized Collection	A structured group of data used for training and evaluation	A folder of labeled images
Training Data	Learning Input	Data used to teach the AI model during training	Thousands of sentences for a language model
Validation Data	Performance Check	Data used to tune the model during training without directly learning from it	Helps prevent overfitting
Test Data	Final Evaluation	Data used to measure how well the model performs after training	New unseen examples
Structured Data	Organized Format	Data arranged in tables with clear categories	Spreadsheets, databases
Unstructured Data	Flexible Format	Data without a predefined structure	Text documents, images, videos
Labeled Data	Guided Learning	Data tagged with correct answers to guide training	Image labeled "cat" or "dog"
Unlabeled Data	Self-Learning Input	Data without labels, used in unsupervised learning	Raw text without categories
Data Quality	Accuracy Measure	The reliability and correctness of data	Clean, complete, and consistent data
Data Bias	Imbalance Issue	When data does not represent all groups fairly	Skewed or incomplete datasets
Data Preprocessing	Preparation Step	Cleaning and organizing data before training	Removing errors, formatting text

The Data Family reminds us that artificial intelligence is only as strong as the information it learns from. High-quality data leads to meaningful insights, while poor data can limit or misguide intelligent systems.

Memory Family Introduction

The Memory Family represents how artificial intelligence systems store, retain, and retrieve information. Just as humans rely on memory to recall past experiences, learn new concepts, and make decisions, AI systems depend on memory to access previously processed information and maintain context.

In artificial intelligence, memory is not a single component but a collection of mechanisms that allow systems to handle information over time. Some forms of memory are short-term, holding information temporarily while a task is being completed. Other forms are long-term, storing learned knowledge that can be used across different tasks and interactions.

Memory plays a critical role in enabling AI systems to understand sequences, maintain context in conversations, and improve decision-making. For example, when a user interacts with a language model, the system uses memory to keep track of previous words, sentences, or prompts in order to generate coherent and relevant responses.

The Memory Family works closely with the Data Family, which provides the information to be stored, and the Parameter Family, which encodes learned knowledge within the model. It also supports the Neural Network Family by enabling systems to process sequences and retain important patterns over time.

Understanding the Memory Family helps students see that AI is not simply reacting to individual inputs in isolation. Instead, it relies on stored information and contextual awareness to produce meaningful and consistent outputs.

In simple terms, if data is what AI learns from, memory is how AI remembers and uses what it has learned.

Memory Family Breakdown Chart

Component	Role	Description	Example
Memory	Information Storage	The ability of an AI system to store and access information	Retaining previous inputs in a task
Short-Term Memory	Temporary Storage	Holds information for immediate processing	Keeping track of words in a sentence
Long-Term Memory	Persistent Storage	Stores learned knowledge for future use	Knowledge embedded in model parameters
Context Memory	Conversation Tracking	Maintains information within a specific interaction	Remembering earlier parts of a prompt
Working Memory	Active Processing	Handles information currently being used in computation	Processing a sequence step by step
External Memory	Extended Storage	Memory stored outside the model for retrieval	Databases, vector stores

Component	Role	Description	Example
Internal Memory	Embedded Knowledge	Information stored within the model itself	Learned patterns inside neural networks
Sequence Memory	Order Awareness	Tracks the order of inputs over time	Understanding sentence structure
Retrieval Mechanism	Access System	Retrieves stored information when needed	Searching relevant past data
Attention Mechanism	Focus System	Highlights important parts of memory for processing	Focusing on key words in a sentence
Memory Capacity	Storage Limit	The amount of information the system can handle at once	Context window size

The Memory Family shows that intelligence is not just about processing information in the moment, but about retaining, organizing, and using knowledge over time to create meaningful understanding.

Knowledge Family Introduction

The Knowledge Family represents how artificial intelligence organizes, connects, and uses information to create understanding. While data provides raw information and memory stores it, knowledge is what gives that information meaning and structure.

In artificial intelligence, knowledge is not simply a collection of facts. It is the result of identifying relationships, patterns, and connections within data. AI systems use knowledge to recognize concepts, make decisions, and generate meaningful responses. This allows machines to move beyond simple data processing and toward more intelligent behavior.

Knowledge can be represented in different ways within AI systems. Some forms are structured, such as databases and knowledge graphs, where relationships between concepts are clearly defined. Other forms are learned implicitly through neural networks, where patterns are encoded within parameters and used to guide predictions.

The Knowledge Family works closely with the Data Family, which provides the information needed to build knowledge, and the Memory Family, which stores and retrieves that information. It also connects with the Parameter Family, where learned knowledge is embedded within the model, and the Neural Network Family, which processes and organizes that knowledge.

Understanding the Knowledge Family helps students recognize that AI systems do not simply memorize information. Instead, they learn how pieces of information relate to one another, allowing them to interpret meaning, solve problems, and respond intelligently.

In simple terms, if data is information and memory stores it, knowledge is the understanding that makes it useful.

Knowledge Family Breakdown Chart

Component	Role	Description	Example
Knowledge	Understanding System	Organized information that allows AI to interpret meaning and make decisions	Recognizing relationships between concepts
Facts	Basic Information	Individual pieces of information stored within a system	"Water freezes at 0°C"
Relationships	Connection Mapping	Links between pieces of information that create meaning	"Teacher teaches student"
Knowledge Representation	Structure System	Methods used to organize and store knowledge in AI	Knowledge graphs, semantic networks
Knowledge Graph	Network Mapping	A structured representation of entities and their relationships	Google Knowledge Graph
Semantic Understanding	Meaning Interpretation	The ability to understand meaning behind words and data	Understanding synonyms and context
Inference	Reasoning Process	Drawing conclusions based on known information	If A = B and B = C, then A = C
Rules	Decision Framework	Logical guidelines used to make decisions	If temperature < 0°C → freeze
Ontology	Concept Framework	A structured system defining categories and relationships	Classification of animals
Explicit Knowledge	Direct Information	Clearly defined and stored knowledge	Rules, databases
Implicit Knowledge	Learned Patterns	Knowledge learned through experience and data	Patterns learned by neural networks
Knowledge Integration	System Coordination	Combining information from multiple sources	Merging text, images, and data

The Knowledge Family transforms information into understanding, allowing artificial intelligence to move beyond data and memory into meaningful reasoning and intelligent decision-making.

AI Model Family Introduction

The AI Model Family represents the core system within artificial intelligence that performs tasks such as prediction, classification, and content generation. It is the part of AI that users interact with, whether they are asking questions, generating images, or analyzing data.

An AI model is a trained system that has learned patterns from data. During training, the model processes large amounts of information and adjusts its internal parameters to improve accuracy. Once trained, the model can take new input and produce meaningful output based on what it has learned.

AI models can take many forms depending on their purpose. Some models are designed to recognize images, others to understand language, and others to make decisions or predictions. Large Language Models (LLMs), for example, are designed to process and generate human language by predicting sequences of tokens.

The AI Model Family works closely with the Data Family, which provides the learning material, and the Parameter Family, which stores learned patterns. It also relies on the Neural Network Family for structure and the Chip and Infrastructure Families for execution and deployment.

Understanding the AI Model Family helps students see that AI is not just a concept, but a working system that has been trained to perform specific tasks. It is the engine that transforms input into output.

In simple terms, if AI is the system, the model is the part that actually does the thinking and producing.

AI Model Family Breakdown Chart

Component	Role	Description	Example
AI Model	Core System	The trained system that performs tasks	Chatbot, image generator
Training	Learning Process	Process of teaching the model using data	Learning from datasets
Inference	Output Generation	Using the trained model to produce results	Answering a question
Model Architecture	Structural Design	Defines how the model is built	Neural networks, transformers
Parameters	Learned Values	Internal values adjusted during training	Billions of weights
Input Data	Entry Information	Data provided to the model for processing	User prompt
Output Data	Result	The response or prediction generated	AI-generated text

Component	Role	Description	Example
Model Types	Functional Categories	Different kinds of models for different tasks	Classification, generation
Fine-Tuning	Model Adjustment	Improving a model for specific tasks	Custom-trained AI
Pretrained Model	Base System	A model trained on large datasets before use	General-purpose AI
Evaluation	Performance Check	Measuring how well the model performs	Accuracy, loss metrics

The AI Model Family represents the working core of artificial intelligence, where learned patterns are transformed into meaningful actions, predictions, and responses.

Neural Network Family Introduction

The Neural Network Family represents the structural foundation of how artificial intelligence learns and processes information. Inspired by the human brain, neural networks are systems of interconnected units, often called neurons, that work together to analyze data, recognize patterns, and make decisions.

In artificial intelligence, a neural network is made up of layers. The input layer receives data, the hidden layers process that data, and the output layer produces a result. As information flows through these layers, the network applies mathematical transformations that allow it to detect patterns and relationships within the data.

Neural networks rely heavily on the Parameter Family, where weights and biases determine how strongly information flows between neurons. During training, these parameters are adjusted to improve the network's performance. The more the network learns, the better it becomes at recognizing patterns and making accurate predictions.

The Neural Network Family works closely with the Data Family, which provides the information needed for learning, and the Memory and Knowledge Families, which help store and organize learned information. It also supports the Token Family when processing language, allowing AI systems to interpret sequences of tokens in meaningful ways.

Understanding neural networks helps students see that AI is not simply following instructions. Instead, it is learning from examples and improving over time through layered processing and pattern recognition.

In simple terms, neural networks are the systems that allow AI to think, learn, and make sense of information.

Neural Network Family Breakdown Chart

Component	Role	Description	Example
Neural Network	Learning Structure	A system of interconnected neurons that processes data and learns patterns	Image recognition system
Neuron (Node)	Processing Unit	A basic unit that receives input, processes it, and passes output forward	A single calculation point
Input Layer	Data Entry Point	The first layer that receives raw data	Pixels of an image
Hidden Layers	Processing Layers	Intermediate layers that transform data and detect patterns	Feature detection layers
Output Layer	Result Generator	The final layer that produces predictions or decisions	"Cat" vs "Dog" classification
Weights	Signal Strength	Values that determine how strongly inputs influence outputs	Higher weight = stronger impact
Bias	Adjustment Value	Helps shift outputs to improve learning accuracy	Fine-tuning predictions
Activation Function	Decision Function	Determines whether a neuron should activate based on input	ReLU, Sigmoid
Forward Propagation	Data Flow	The process of passing input data through the network to produce output	Input → Hidden → Output
Backpropagation	Learning Process	Adjusts weights and biases based on error to improve performance	Correcting mistakes
Loss Function	Error Measurement	Calculates how far the output is from the correct answer	Prediction vs actual
Deep Neural Network	Advanced Structure	A network with many hidden layers for complex learning	Deep learning models

The Neural Network Family provides the structure that allows artificial intelligence to transform data into understanding, making it possible for machines to learn from experience and improve over time.

AI Translator Architecture Family Introduction

The AI Translator Architecture Family represents the system that transforms input into meaningful output in artificial intelligence. It acts as the bridge between what humans provide and what AI produces. Whether a user types a question, uploads an image, or speaks a command, this architecture is responsible for interpreting that input and generating a response.

In artificial intelligence, translation does not only mean converting one language to another. It refers to the broader process of transforming one form of information into another. For example, text can be translated into a response, speech can be converted into text, and images can be interpreted into descriptions. This transformation process is at the core of how modern AI systems function.

The AI Translator Architecture is built on multiple foundational families. It relies on the Token Family to break input into manageable units, the Neural Network Family to process patterns, and the Parameter Family to guide learning. It also uses knowledge and memory to maintain context and produce coherent results.

At the center of this architecture is the ability to encode and decode information. Encoding transforms input into a format the model can understand, while decoding converts processed information back into human-readable output. This continuous transformation allows AI systems to interact with users in a natural and meaningful way.

Understanding the AI Translator Architecture Family helps students see that AI is not simply responding randomly. Instead, it is systematically translating input into output through structured processes and learned patterns.

In simple terms, if tokens are the language pieces and neural networks are the brain, the AI Translator Architecture is the system that turns understanding into communication.

AI Translator Architecture Family Breakdown Chart

Component	Role	Description	Example
AI Translator Architecture	Transformation System	Converts input into meaningful output	Question → Answer
Input Processing	Data Intake	Receives and prepares user input for analysis	Text prompt entered by a user
Encoding	Input Conversion	Transforms input into numerical representations	Words → token IDs
Context Building	Meaning Formation	Organizes input into a structured understanding	Sentence context tracking
Sequence Processing	Order Handling	Maintains the correct order of information	Word sequence in a sentence
Attention Mechanism	Focus System	Identifies important parts of input data	Highlighting key words
Representation Layer	Feature Mapping	Converts data into internal representations for processing	Embeddings
Decoding	Output Generation	Converts processed data back into human-readable form	Token IDs → words

Component	Role	Description	Example
Output Generation	Response Creation	Produces the final answer or result	AI-generated response
Multimodal Translation	Cross-Format Processing	Translates between different types of data	Image → text description
Feedback Loop	Improvement Cycle	Uses results to refine future outputs	Model learning over time

The AI Translator Architecture Family shows that artificial intelligence is not just about understanding information, but about transforming it into meaningful communication that humans can use and interact with.

AI Architecture Family Introduction

The AI Architecture Family represents the overall design and structure of an artificial intelligence system. While individual families such as Data, Parameters, and Neural Networks explain how AI learns and processes information, the AI Architecture Family shows how all these components are organized and work together as a complete system.

In artificial intelligence, architecture refers to the blueprint that defines how data flows through a system, how components interact, and how decisions are produced. It determines how input is received, how it is processed, and how output is generated. A well-designed architecture allows AI systems to operate efficiently, scale to large problems, and produce reliable results.

AI architectures can vary depending on the type of system being built. Some are designed for image recognition, others for language processing, and others for decision-making or automation. Despite these differences, most architectures share common elements such as input layers, processing layers, memory components, and output mechanisms.

The AI Architecture Family connects all foundational families. It integrates the Data Family for input, the Token Family for language processing, the Neural Network Family for computation, the Parameter Family for learning, and the Memory and Knowledge Families for storing and organizing information. It also works closely with the AI Translator Architecture Family to transform input into meaningful output.

Understanding the AI Architecture Family helps students see the "big picture" of artificial intelligence. Instead of viewing AI as separate parts, they begin to understand it as a coordinated system where each component plays a specific role.

In simple terms, if individual families are the parts of AI, the AI Architecture Family is the blueprint that brings everything together into one working system.

AI Architecture Family Breakdown Chart

Component	Role	Description	Example
AI Architecture	System Blueprint	The overall design that defines how an AI system is structured and operates	ChatGPT system design
Input Layer	Data Entry Point	Receives raw input from users or external sources	Text prompt, image upload
Preprocessing Layer	Data Preparation	Cleans and organizes input data before processing	Tokenization, normalization
Processing Core	Computation Engine	The main system where data is analyzed and transformed	Neural networks, transformers
Parameter System	Learning Core	Stores adjustable values that guide learning and predictions	Model weights and biases
Memory System	Context Storage	Maintains and retrieves information during processing	Context window, external memory
Knowledge System	Understanding Layer	Organizes relationships and meaning within the system	Knowledge graphs, learned patterns
Decision Layer	Output Logic	Determines the final output based on processed data	Selecting the best response
Output Layer	Result Delivery	Presents results to the user in a usable format	Text, image, or audio response
Feedback Loop	Improvement System	Uses outcomes to refine future performance	Model updates and retraining
Scalability System	Expansion Capability	Allows the system to handle increasing data and complexity	Cloud-based AI systems
Integration Layer	System Connection	Connects AI with external tools and platforms	APIs, databases, applications

The AI Architecture Family reveals that artificial intelligence is not a single technology, but a coordinated system of interconnected components working together to transform data into intelligent outcomes.

Chip Family Introduction

The Chip Family represents the physical hardware that powers artificial intelligence systems. While software components such as data, algorithms, and neural networks define how AI works, none of these systems can function without the computing chips that perform the actual calculations.

Chips are specialized electronic components designed to process information at extremely high speeds. In artificial intelligence, these chips handle the complex mathematical operations required for training models and generating outputs. Every prediction, calculation, and response produced by an AI system is executed by hardware within the Chip Family.

Different types of chips are used depending on the needs of the system. Central Processing Units (CPUs) handle general-purpose tasks, while Graphics Processing Units (GPUs) are optimized for parallel processing, making them ideal for training neural networks. More specialized chips, such as Tensor Processing Units (TPUs) and Neural Processing Units (NPUs), are designed specifically for AI workloads, enabling faster and more efficient computation.

The Chip Family works closely with the Neural Network Family, which defines the structure of computation, and the Parameter Family, which stores the values being processed. It also connects to the Infrastructure Family, where large-scale systems of chips are organized in data centers and cloud environments.

Understanding the Chip Family helps students recognize that artificial intelligence is not purely abstract. It depends on physical machines that require power, resources, and engineering to operate. These chips are the engines that bring AI models to life.

In simple terms, if AI is the intelligence, chips are the machines that make that intelligence possible.

Chip Family Breakdown Chart

Component	Role	Description	Example
Chip (Processor)	Computation Engine	Electronic hardware that performs calculations required for AI	CPU, GPU
CPU (Central Processing Unit)	General Processor	Handles a wide range of computing tasks	Running basic applications
GPU (Graphics Processing Unit)	Parallel Processor	Processes many calculations at once, ideal for AI training	Training neural networks
TPU (Tensor Processing Unit)	AI Accelerator	Specialized chip designed for machine learning tasks	Google TPU
NPU (Neural Processing Unit)	Edge AI Processor	Optimized for running AI on devices like phones	Smartphone AI features
AI Accelerator	Performance Booster	Hardware designed to speed up AI computations	Dedicated AI chips
Memory (Hardware)	Data Storage	Stores data and instructions for processing	RAM, VRAM

Component	Role	Description	Example
Parallel Processing	Speed Mechanism	Ability to perform multiple calculations simultaneously	GPUs processing thousands of operations
Throughput	Processing Capacity	Amount of data processed over time	High-performance computing systems
Latency	Response Time	Time it takes to process a request	Faster chips = lower latency
Power Consumption	Energy Usage	Amount of energy required to run the chip	High-performance GPUs use more power
Edge Devices	Local Processing	Devices that run AI locally without cloud support	Phones, smart cameras

The Chip Family reminds us that behind every intelligent system is powerful hardware performing millions or billions of calculations, turning abstract models into real-world functionality.

Watts Family Introduction

The Watts Family represents the measurement of power used by artificial intelligence systems. While the Chip Family provides the hardware that performs computations, the Watts Family explains how much energy those systems consume while operating.

A watt is a unit of power that measures the rate at which energy is used. In artificial intelligence, watts help us understand how much electricity is required to run processors, train models, and generate responses. Every time an AI system processes data, performs calculations, or produces output, it consumes power.

Different AI systems require different levels of power depending on their size and complexity. Small systems, such as those running on mobile devices, use relatively low amounts of power. In contrast, large-scale AI models operating in data centers can require significant amounts of electricity, especially during training, where billions of calculations are performed continuously.

The Watts Family works closely with the Chip Family, which determines how efficiently computations are performed, and the Infrastructure Family, where large networks of machines operate together. It also connects to the overall design of AI systems, as more efficient models can reduce power consumption while maintaining performance.

Understanding the Watts Family helps students recognize that artificial intelligence is not only about intelligence and computation, but also about energy use and resource management. As AI continues to grow, managing power efficiently becomes an important part of building responsible and sustainable systems.

In simple terms, if chips perform the work, watts measure how much power it takes to do that work.

Watts Family Breakdown Chart

Component	Role	Description	Example
Watt (W)	Power Measurement	Unit that measures the rate of energy use	A device using 100 watts
Power Consumption	Energy Usage Rate	Amount of power used during operation	AI model running on GPUs
Energy Efficiency	Performance Balance	How effectively a system uses power to perform tasks	More output with less power
High-Performance Computing	Intensive Power Use	Systems that require large amounts of power for complex tasks	AI training clusters
Idle Power	Standby Usage	Power consumed when systems are not actively processing	Servers waiting for requests
Peak Power	Maximum Usage	Highest level of power used during heavy workloads	Training large AI models
Thermal Output	Heat Generation	Heat produced as a result of power usage	Cooling systems in data centers
Cooling Systems	Temperature Control	Systems used to manage heat from high power usage	Air or liquid cooling
Power Supply	Energy Source	Provides electricity to AI systems	Electrical grid, batteries
Edge Power Usage	Local Energy Use	Power consumption on smaller devices	Smartphones, IoT devices
Data Center Power	Large-Scale Usage	Power required for large AI operations	Server farms running AI models
Sustainable Energy	Efficiency Goal	Use of renewable energy to reduce environmental impact	Solar-powered data centers

The Watts Family highlights that intelligence comes with a cost—every AI system requires power, and understanding that power is essential for building efficient and sustainable technologies.

Watts Family (AI Power Usage Scale)

Definition

The **Watts Family** represents the real-time power usage of artificial intelligence systems, measured in watts (W). It shows how much power AI systems consume at a given moment as they process data and perform computations.

Watts Scale

1 Watt
10 Watts
100 Watts
500 Watts
1,000 Watts (1 Kilowatt)
10,000 Watts (10 Kilowatts)
100,000 Watts (100 Kilowatts)
1,000,000 Watts (1 Megawatt)
10,000,000 Watts (10 Megawatts)
100,000,000+ Watts (100+ Megawatts)

Key Characteristics

Measured in real-world electrical power

Higher watt values indicate higher processing demand

Used to represent the scale of AI systems from small devices to large infrastructures

Closely connected to the Chip Family, Energy Family, and Infrastructure Family

Examples

Low watts → small devices and basic AI functions

Medium watts → computers and advanced applications

High watts → data centers and large AI systems

Summary

The **Watts Family** provides a numerical representation of how much power artificial intelligence systems use in real time, helping to illustrate the scale and intensity of AI operations.

🪨 Student Insight

Watts show how much power AI is using right now.

AI Energy Family Introduction

The AI Energy Family represents the total amount of energy consumed by artificial intelligence systems over time. While the Watts Family measures the rate at which power is used at any given moment, the Energy Family focuses on the accumulated energy required to perform tasks, run systems, and sustain operations.

In artificial intelligence, energy is used every time a model is trained, a system processes data, or a response is generated. Large-scale AI systems, especially those operating in data centers, can consume significant amounts of energy due to the continuous processing of massive datasets and complex computations.

Energy is typically measured over time using units such as kilowatt-hours (kWh), which reflect how much power has been used during a specific period. For example, running a high-performance AI system for several hours or days results in a total energy cost that goes beyond the moment-to-moment power usage measured in watts.

The AI Energy Family works closely with the Watts Family, which provides the rate of power consumption, and the Chip Family, which determines how efficiently computations are performed. It also connects to the Infrastructure Family, where large-scale systems operate continuously and require long-term energy management.

Understanding the AI Energy Family helps students recognize that artificial intelligence has real-world resource implications. It is not only about performance and speed, but also about sustainability, efficiency, and responsible use of technology.

In simple terms, if watts measure how fast energy is used, energy measures how much is used over time.

AI Energy Family Breakdown Chart

Component	Role	Description	Example
Energy	Total Consumption	The total amount of power used over a period of time	Running an AI system for hours or days
Kilowatt-hour (kWh)	Energy Measurement	Unit used to measure energy consumption over time	1 kWh = using 1,000 watts for 1 hour
Energy Usage	Consumption Tracking	Total energy required for AI operations	Training a large model
Training Energy	Learning Cost	Energy used during model training processes	Weeks of GPU usage
Inference Energy	Response Cost	Energy used when AI generates outputs	Answering a user prompt

Component	Role	Description	Example
Energy Efficiency	Optimization Goal	Reducing energy use while maintaining performance	Efficient AI models
Energy Scaling	Growth Impact	Increase in energy use as systems grow larger	Bigger models = more energy
Data Center Energy	Infrastructure Demand	Total energy used by large AI facilities	Server farms operating 24/7
Cooling Energy	Temperature Control	Energy required to cool systems and prevent overheating	Air conditioning in data centers
Renewable Energy	Sustainability Source	Use of clean energy to power AI systems	Solar, wind-powered data centers
Carbon Impact	Environmental Effect	Emissions associated with energy consumption	AI training carbon footprint
Energy Management	Resource Control	Strategies to monitor and reduce energy use	Efficient scheduling, hardware optimization

The AI Energy Family reminds us that artificial intelligence operates within the physical world, where every computation consumes energy and every system has an impact on resources and sustainability.

Energy Family (Total Power Consumption of Artificial Intelligence)

Definition

The **Energy Family** represents the total amount of electricity used by artificial intelligence systems over time. It is measured in watt-hours (Wh) or kilowatt-hours (kWh) and shows how much energy AI systems consume while running.

Energy Scale

1 Watt-hour (Wh)
10 Watt-hours (Wh)
100 Watt-hours (Wh)
500 Watt-hours (Wh)
1,000 Watt-hours (1 Kilowatt-hour, kWh)
10,000 Watt-hours (10 kWh)
100,000 Watt-hours (100 kWh)
1,000,000 Watt-hours (1 Megawatt-hour, MWh)
10,000,000 Watt-hours (10 MWh)
100,000,000+ Watt-hours (100+ MWh)

Key Characteristics

Measured over time (not instant like watts)

Represents total electricity consumption

Increases the longer AI systems run

Directly related to cost and energy usage

Closely connected to Watts Family, Chip Family, and Infrastructure Family

Examples

Low energy → short AI tasks or small devices

Medium energy → daily AI usage on computers

High energy → training AI models and running data centers

Summary

The **Energy Family** provides a numerical representation of the total electricity consumed by artificial intelligence systems over time, helping to illustrate the overall cost and impact of AI operations.

🧠 Student Insight

Energy shows how much total power AI has used over time.

AI Infrastructure Family Introduction

The AI Infrastructure Family represents the large-scale systems and environments that support, power, and connect artificial intelligence technologies. While individual components such as chips, data, and models explain how AI works, infrastructure explains where and how these systems operate in the real world.

AI infrastructure includes data centers, cloud platforms, networking systems, and storage environments that allow artificial intelligence to function at scale. These systems provide the computing power, data access, and connectivity needed to train models, process information, and deliver results to users around the world.

Modern AI systems rely heavily on cloud-based infrastructure, where thousands of machines work together to handle massive workloads. This allows AI to scale efficiently, making it possible to process large datasets, run complex models, and serve millions of users simultaneously. Infrastructure also ensures reliability, security, and continuous availability of AI services.

The AI Infrastructure Family works closely with the Chip Family, which provides the hardware, the Watts and Energy Families, which manage power consumption, and the Data Family, which supplies the information being processed. It also supports the AI Architecture Family by providing the environment where all system components are deployed and connected.

Understanding the AI Infrastructure Family helps students recognize that artificial intelligence is not contained within a single device. Instead, it operates across global systems that require coordination, resources, and engineering to function effectively.

In simple terms, if AI is the system and chips are the engines, infrastructure is the environment that allows everything to run at scale.

AI Infrastructure Family Breakdown Chart

Component	Role	Description	Example
AI Infrastructure	System Environment	The physical and digital systems that support AI operations	Global AI platforms
Data Center	Processing Hub	Facilities that house servers and computing equipment	Large server farms
Cloud Computing	Scalable Platform	Remote systems that provide computing resources over the internet	AWS, Azure, Google Cloud
Servers	Compute Units	Machines that process data and run AI models	Rack-mounted servers
Networking	Connectivity System	Systems that allow communication between machines	Internet, fiber networks
Storage Systems	Data Management	Systems that store large volumes of data	Databases, cloud storage
Distributed Computing	Workload Sharing	Splitting tasks across multiple machines for efficiency	Parallel processing across clusters
Edge Infrastructure	Local Processing	Running AI closer to the user or device	Smart devices, IoT systems
Load Balancing	Traffic Control	Distributes workloads to prevent overload	Managing user requests
Security Systems	Protection Layer	Safeguards data and systems from threats	Encryption, firewalls
Redundancy	Reliability System	Backup systems to ensure continuous operation	Failover servers

Component	Role	Description	Example
Scalability	Growth Capability	Ability to expand resources as demand increases	Adding more servers dynamically

The AI Infrastructure Family reveals that artificial intelligence operates on a global scale, relying on interconnected systems that provide the power, storage, and connectivity needed to support intelligent technologies.

AI Agent Family Introduction

The AI Agent Family represents systems that can take action, make decisions, and perform tasks on behalf of users or other systems. Unlike traditional AI models that only respond to input, AI agents are designed to operate with a level of autonomy, allowing them to plan, execute, and adapt to achieve specific goals.

An AI agent receives input from its environment, processes that information, and takes actions based on predefined objectives or learned behaviors. These actions can include answering questions, automating workflows, retrieving information, or interacting with other systems. Some agents operate in simple environments, while others function in complex systems that require continuous decision-making.

AI agents often combine multiple foundational families. They use the Data Family to gather information, the Memory and Knowledge Families to retain and understand context, and the Neural Network and Parameter Families to process and learn from interactions. They also rely on the AI Architecture and Infrastructure Families to operate reliably at scale.

Modern AI agents can work independently or as part of larger systems. For example, a customer support agent can respond to inquiries automatically, while a more advanced agent can complete multi-step tasks such as scheduling, research, or system management.

Understanding the AI Agent Family helps students see that artificial intelligence is not only about generating responses, but also about taking meaningful action in real-world scenarios.

In simple terms, if AI models think and respond, AI agents act and execute.

AI Agent Family Breakdown Chart

Component	Role	Description	Example
AI Agent	Action System	An AI system that can make decisions and perform tasks	Virtual assistant

Component	Role	Description	Example
Environment	Operating Context	The space where the agent interacts and gathers information	Web, apps, databases
Input Perception	Data Intake	Receives information from the environment	User query or sensor input
Decision Engine	Action Selection	Determines what action to take based on input	Choosing a response or task
Action Execution	Task Performance	Carries out decisions in the environment	Sending an email, retrieving data
Goal System	Objective Setting	Defines what the agent is trying to achieve	Complete a task or solve a problem
Planning Module	Strategy Builder	Breaks down tasks into steps	Multi-step problem solving
Feedback Loop	Learning Cycle	Improves performance based on outcomes	Adjusting actions over time
Autonomy Level	Independence Scale	Degree of independence in decision-making	Fully automated vs assisted
Multi-Agent System	Collaboration Network	Multiple agents working together	Coordinated AI systems

Ingredient Family Introduction

The Ingredient Family represents the essential components that come together to create an artificial intelligence system. Just as a recipe requires specific ingredients to produce a final dish, AI systems rely on a combination of foundational elements working together to function effectively.

Artificial intelligence is not built from a single component. It requires data to learn from, algorithms to guide processing, models to perform tasks, hardware to execute computations, and energy to power the entire system. Each of these elements plays a critical role, and the absence of any one component would prevent the system from operating properly.

The Ingredient Family provides a simplified way for students to understand AI as a system made up of interconnected parts. Instead of viewing AI as complex or mysterious, learners can begin to see it as something constructed from identifiable and understandable components.

This family connects directly with all other foundational families, including Data, Algorithm, Neural Network, Parameter, Chip, and Energy Families. It serves as an overview that brings these elements together into a unified perspective.

Understanding the Ingredient Family helps students recognize that artificial intelligence is built, not magical. It is the result of carefully combining the right components in the right way.

In simple terms, if AI is the final product, the Ingredient Family represents everything needed to build it.

Ingredient Family Breakdown Chart

Component	Role	Description	Example
Data	Learning Input	Provides the information AI uses to learn patterns	Text, images, audio
Algorithms	Instruction Set	Guides how data is processed and decisions are made	Sorting, classification
AI Models	Execution System	Performs tasks such as prediction or generation	Language models
Neural Networks	Processing Structure	Organizes how data is processed through layers	Deep learning models
Parameters	Learning Adjustments	Fine-tune how the model learns and makes predictions	Weights and biases
Tokens	Language Units	Breaks text into smaller pieces for processing	Words or subwords
Hardware (Chips)	Computation Engine	Executes calculations required by AI systems	GPUs, CPUs
Energy	Power Source	Supplies the energy needed to run systems	Electricity usage
Infrastructure	Support System	Provides the environment for AI to operate at scale	Cloud systems, data centers
Memory	Storage System	Stores and retrieves information for processing	Context memory
Knowledge	Understanding Layer	Represents meaning and relationships within data	Knowledge graphs

The Ingredient Family shows that artificial intelligence is built from a combination of essential components, each playing a vital role in creating intelligent systems.

The Frontend and Backend Family of Artificial Intelligence

How AI Systems Connect User Interaction to Intelligent Processing

Introduction

Every artificial intelligence system operates through two essential layers: the frontend and the backend. These layers work together to transform human interaction into intelligent responses, allowing AI systems to function smoothly and effectively.

The frontend is the part of the system that users see and interact with. It includes screens, input tools, and the display of results. Whether a user is typing a question, speaking a command, or uploading an image, all interaction begins at the frontend.

Behind the scenes, the backend serves as the processing engine of the system. It receives input from the frontend, manages data, connects to the AI model, and performs the computations needed to generate a response. The backend is where the intelligence of the system operates, using models, algorithms, and infrastructure to interpret and respond to user requests.

This visual illustrates how these two layers work together as a complete system. It shows the flow of information from user input to AI processing and back to the user as a result. By understanding this structure, students can see that AI is not a single tool, but a coordinated system of layers working together.

In simple terms, the frontend is where interaction happens, and the backend is where intelligence is created.

Every AI system has two sides: what you see and what actually does the thinking.

This structure helps students understand how every interaction with AI is supported by a hidden system of processing and intelligence.

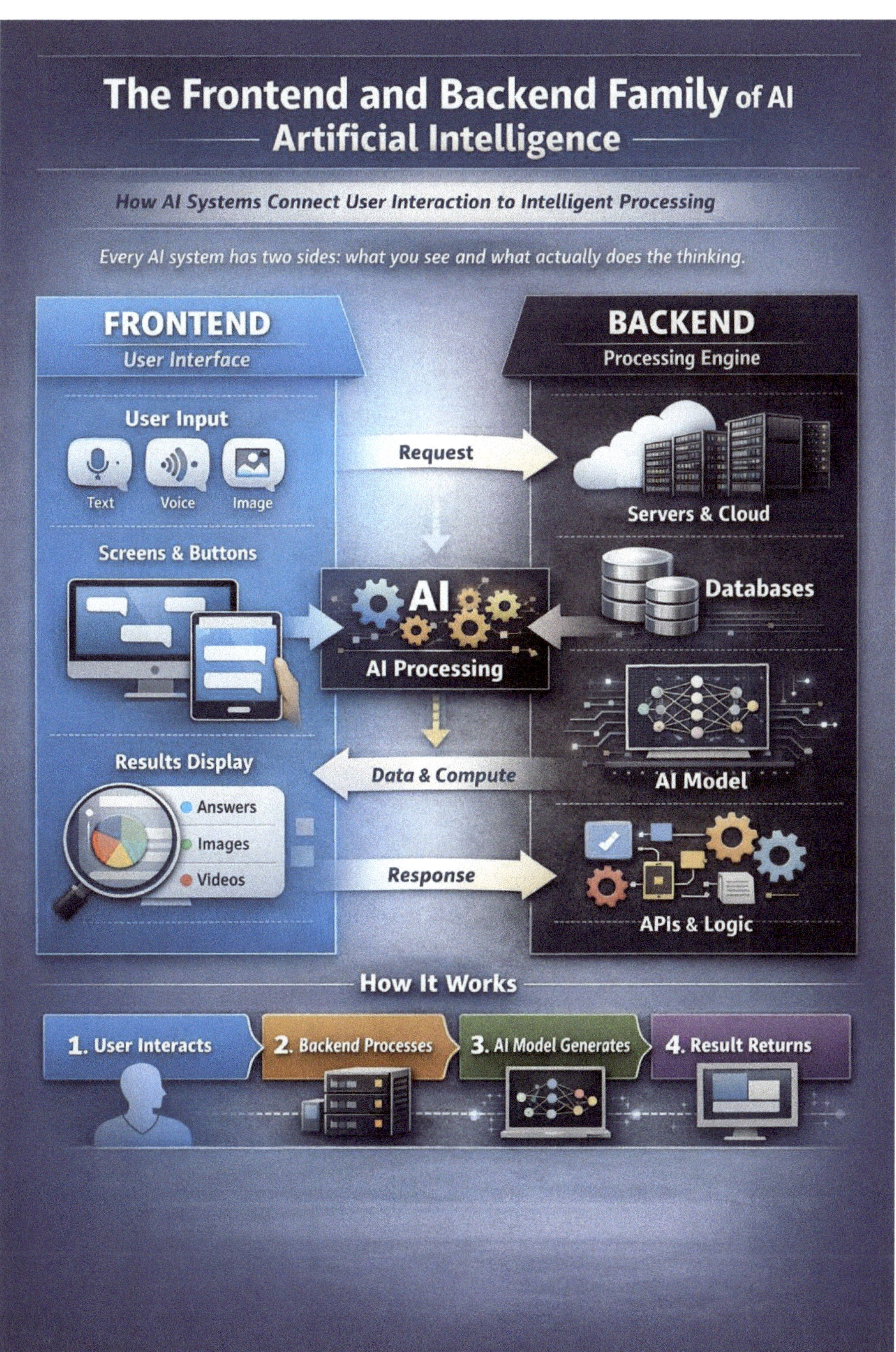

The Frontend and Backend Family of AI
Artificial Intelligence
How AI Systems Connect User Interaction to Intelligent Processing
Every AI system has two sides: what you see and what actually does the thinking.
FRONTEND
User Interface
BACKEND
Processing Engine
User Input
Text
Voice
Image
Request
Servers & Cloud
Screens & Buttons
AI
AI Processing
Databases
Results Display
Data & Compute
AI Model
Answers
Images
Videos
Response
APIs & Logic
How It Works
1. User Interacts
2. Backend Processes
3. AI Model Generates
4. Result Returns

AI Qubit Family Introduction

The AI Qubit Family represents the foundation of quantum computing as it relates to artificial intelligence. While traditional computing relies on bits, which can exist as either 0 or 1, quantum computing uses qubits, which can exist in multiple states simultaneously.

A qubit is the basic unit of quantum information. Unlike classical bits, qubits can take advantage of properties such as superposition and entanglement, allowing quantum systems to process complex computations more efficiently in certain scenarios. This opens new possibilities for solving problems that are difficult or impossible for traditional computers.

In the context of artificial intelligence, qubits have the potential to accelerate learning processes, optimize large-scale systems, and improve complex simulations. Although quantum AI is still in development, it represents a future direction where computational power can expand beyond current limitations.

The AI Qubit Family connects with the Chip Family, as quantum processors are specialized hardware, and with the Algorithm Family, where new types of quantum algorithms are designed. It also relates to the Parameter and Neural Network Families, as researchers explore quantum-enhanced learning models.

Understanding the AI Qubit Family helps students see that artificial intelligence is continuously evolving. It introduces the idea that the foundations of computing themselves can change, leading to new forms of intelligence and problem-solving.

In simple terms, if bits are the foundation of today's computing, qubits represent the foundation of tomorrow's possibilities.

AI Qubit Family Breakdown Chart

Component	Role	Description	Example
Qubit	Quantum Unit	Basic unit of quantum information	Quantum bit in a quantum computer
Superposition	Multi-State Ability	Ability to exist in multiple states at once	0 and 1 simultaneously
Entanglement	Connection Property	Linking qubits so they influence each other	Paired quantum states
Quantum Gate	Operation System	Performs operations on qubits	Quantum logic gates
Quantum Circuit	Processing Structure	Sequence of quantum operations	Quantum algorithms
Quantum Processor	Hardware Engine	Specialized chip for quantum computing	Quantum computer hardware

Component	Role	Description	Example
Quantum Algorithm	Computation Method	Algorithm designed for quantum systems	Optimization problems
Quantum Speedup	Performance Advantage	Faster processing for certain problems	Complex simulations
Quantum Noise	Stability Challenge	Errors caused by environmental interference	Qubit instability
Quantum Error Correction	Stability Solution	Techniques to reduce errors in quantum systems	Fault-tolerant computing

The AI Qubit Family introduces a new frontier in computing, where the limits of traditional systems are expanded, opening the door to more powerful and advanced forms of artificial intelligence.

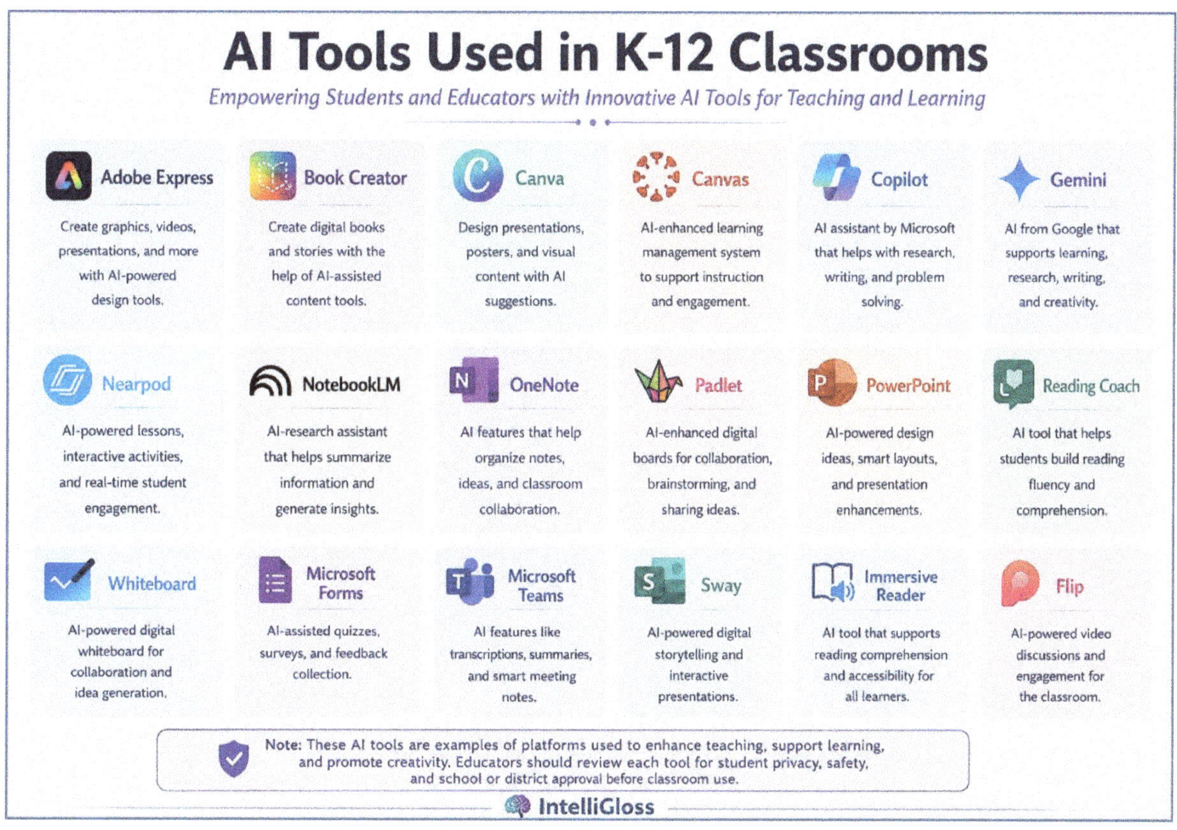

Table of Contents

Reflecting on the role algorithms play in shaping society and the future.

Introduction

The Power of Algorithms: How Computers Solve Problems Step by Step

We live in a world powered by invisible instructions.

Every time you search the internet, open a navigation app, scroll through social media, or watch a recommended video online, a set of step-by-step instructions is quietly working behind the scenes. These instructions guide computers on how to process information, make decisions, and produce useful results. These instructions are called **algorithms**.

Although most people interact with digital technology every day, few stop to think about how these systems actually work. Computers do not think, feel, or understand information the way humans do. Instead, they follow carefully designed procedures created by programmers and engineers. These procedures allow machines to process large amounts of data quickly and accurately.

Algorithms are the foundation of modern computing. They help computers organize information, search for answers, analyze patterns, and solve complex problems. Without algorithms, the digital systems that power our modern world would not function.

Today, algorithms are even more important because they play a central role in **artificial intelligence (AI)**. AI systems rely on algorithms to recognize images, translate languages, recommend music, assist with medical diagnoses, and support scientific research. In many ways, algorithms act as the logical framework that allows intelligent technologies to operate.

Understanding algorithms is not only important for computer scientists and engineers. It is becoming an essential form of **digital literacy** for students, educators, and citizens living in an increasingly technological world. Learning how algorithms work helps us better understand the tools we use every day and allows us to think critically about how technology influences our lives.

This book was written to make the concept of algorithms clear, accessible, and engaging for learners at all levels. Rather than focusing only on technical programming details, the goal of this book is to explain how algorithms function as structured problem-solving systems. Readers will explore how computers follow instructions, how algorithms organize information, and how these systems power everything from search engines to artificial intelligence.

Throughout this book, we will explore questions such as:

- What exactly is an algorithm?
- How do computers follow step-by-step instructions?
- Why are algorithms essential for modern technology?
- How do algorithms power artificial intelligence?
- What ethical challenges arise when algorithms influence decisions?

By the end of this journey, readers will gain a deeper understanding of how computers solve problems and why algorithms play such an important role in the digital world.

The goal of this book is simple: to reveal the hidden logic behind modern technology and help readers understand the powerful systems that quietly shape our everyday lives.

Welcome to the world of algorithms.

Chapter 1: The Invisible Instructions Running the Digital World

Modern life is deeply connected to digital technology. Every day people rely on smartphones, computers, navigation systems, search engines, and intelligent software to help them communicate, learn, and solve problems. Although these technologies appear complex and powerful, they all operate based on a simple underlying principle: computers follow carefully designed instructions. These instructions are known as algorithms. Algorithms operate quietly behind the scenes, guiding machines as they organize information, process data, and produce useful results. Because these instructions are hidden within software systems, most people never see them. Yet they play a central role in nearly every digital activity in the modern world.

When someone types a question into a search engine, the system quickly analyzes billions of web pages and returns the most relevant results in a fraction of a second. When a navigation application calculates the fastest route to a destination, it evaluates traffic patterns, road distances, and travel times. When a streaming platform recommends a movie or song, it analyzes viewing habits and preferences to predict what a user might enjoy. Each of these actions depends on algorithms that guide the computer through a structured set of steps. The user experiences a fast and convenient result, but behind that result is a complex process of digital problem solving.

An algorithm can be understood as a set of instructions designed to solve a specific problem. In everyday life, humans often follow similar step-by-step processes without realizing it. For example, preparing a meal requires a sequence of actions such as gathering ingredients, mixing them in a certain order, cooking at a particular temperature, and serving the final dish. Each step must occur in the proper sequence for the outcome to be successful. In computing, algorithms function in a similar way. They tell a computer exactly what steps to follow in order to transform input data into meaningful output.

Computers rely on algorithms because machines cannot interpret instructions the way humans do. A computer does not possess intuition, understanding, or awareness. Instead, it performs calculations and processes data according to precise instructions written by programmers. These instructions are expressed through programming languages, which are eventually translated into binary code that the computer's hardware can understand. Binary code consists of combinations of zeros and ones, the fundamental digital signals that allow electronic circuits to represent information.

Although algorithms operate through precise mathematical logic, their influence extends far beyond simple calculations. Algorithms shape the way people interact with information, media, and communication networks. For example, social media platforms rely on algorithms to determine which posts appear in a user's feed. These systems analyze factors such as past interactions, popularity of content, and user behavior patterns to decide which information should be displayed first. In this way, algorithms influence what people read, watch, and discuss in their daily lives.

Online shopping platforms also rely heavily on algorithms. When a customer browses products, the system analyzes previous purchases, search history, and similar consumer behavior to recommend items that might be appealing. This process is often called a recommendation system. By studying patterns in large collections of data, algorithms can make predictions about preferences and behavior. These predictions help businesses personalize experiences for millions of users simultaneously.

Navigation systems provide another clear example of algorithms in action. When a driver enters a destination into a GPS application, the system analyzes maps, road networks, traffic data, and estimated travel times. The algorithm compares multiple possible routes and calculates which one will lead to the destination most efficiently. As traffic conditions change, the algorithm may adjust the route to provide a faster path. The driver experiences a smooth navigation experience, but the computer is constantly performing calculations in the background.

Search engines represent one of the most powerful applications of algorithms. When a user searches for information online, the search engine must analyze enormous collections of web pages and rank them according to relevance and quality. This process involves algorithms that evaluate keywords, website structure, user behavior, and other factors. The result is a ranked list of pages that appear most likely to answer the user's question. The speed and accuracy of this process depend on the efficiency of the underlying algorithms.

In recent years, algorithms have also become central to the development of artificial intelligence. AI systems use algorithms to analyze patterns in large datasets and learn from examples. These algorithms allow machines to recognize images, translate languages, and respond to questions. While these systems may appear intelligent, they are still operating through mathematical models and structured procedures designed by humans. The algorithms enable the machine to process large volumes of data and identify patterns that might be difficult for humans to detect.

Understanding algorithms is an important step toward developing digital literacy. As technology becomes more deeply integrated into society, it is essential for people to understand how these systems function and how they influence decision making. Algorithms affect areas such as healthcare, education, transportation, finance, and communication. By learning how algorithms work, students gain insight into the logical foundations of modern technology and develop the ability to think critically about digital systems.

One of the most valuable skills students can develop is algorithmic thinking. This type of thinking involves breaking a complex problem into smaller, manageable steps that can be solved in sequence. When individuals learn to approach problems in this structured way, they become better equipped to design solutions, analyze processes, and understand how technology operates. Algorithmic thinking is not limited to computer science; it can also be applied to everyday problem solving in many different fields.

The digital world may appear mysterious or complicated, but at its core it is built upon simple logical principles. Algorithms provide the structure that allows computers to organize information, analyze data, and perform useful tasks. Although users may never see the instructions directly, these invisible systems operate continuously in the background of modern technology. By exploring how algorithms function, students begin to uncover the hidden mechanisms that power the digital world.

As this book progresses, readers will learn how algorithms are designed, how computers execute them, and how different types of algorithms solve different kinds of problems. From organizing information to powering artificial intelligence, algorithms form the logical backbone of modern computing. Understanding them opens the door to a deeper appreciation of the technology that shapes our world and prepares students to participate in the evolving digital future.

Chapter 1 Summary

Chapter 1 introduced the idea that much of the modern digital world operates through invisible systems of instructions known as algorithms. Although people interact with computers, phones, and online platforms every day, they rarely see the step-by-step processes that allow these systems to function. Algorithms provide the logical structure that computers use to organize information, process data, and produce results.

An algorithm is a sequence of clearly defined instructions designed to solve a problem or complete a task. Computers rely on algorithms because they cannot think or reason like humans. Instead, they follow exact procedures written by programmers and engineers. These procedures guide the computer through calculations, comparisons, and decisions that eventually lead to a useful output.

The chapter explained that algorithms are present in many everyday technologies. Search engines use algorithms to find and rank information across billions of websites. Navigation systems rely on algorithms to determine the fastest route between locations. Social media platforms use algorithms to decide which posts appear in a user's feed. Online shopping systems analyze customer behavior through algorithms in order to recommend products.

Algorithms also form the foundation of artificial intelligence systems. AI technologies analyze large amounts of data in order to recognize patterns, generate predictions, and support decision making. While these systems may appear intelligent, they still operate through mathematical models and structured procedures.

Understanding algorithms helps people develop digital literacy. By learning how these systems function, students gain insight into the logic behind modern technology and become better prepared to analyze the systems that shape everyday life. Algorithmic thinking encourages individuals to break complex problems into smaller steps, an approach that is useful not only in computing but in many areas of learning and problem solving.

As the book continues, readers will explore how algorithms are designed, how computers execute instructions, and how different types of algorithms solve different types of problems.

Reflection Questions

1. Why are algorithms considered "invisible instructions" in modern technology?
2. Think about a digital tool you use every day. What type of problem do you think its algorithms are solving?
3. Why do computers need algorithms in order to function properly?
4. How might understanding algorithms help people become more informed users of technology?
5. In what ways could algorithms influence the information people see online?

Worksheet: Understanding Algorithms

Part A: Concept Identification

Write a short definition for each of the following terms based on what you learned in the chapter.

1. Algorithm
2. Input
3. Output
4. Digital system
5. Artificial intelligence

Part B: Everyday Algorithms

Many everyday activities follow step-by-step instructions similar to algorithms. Describe the steps involved in one of the following activities.

Choose one:

Making a sandwich
Preparing for school in the morning
Logging into an online account

Write the steps in order as if you were giving instructions to a computer.

Step 1:
Step 2:
Step 3:
Step 4:
Step 5:

Part C: Technology and Algorithms

Match each technology with the problem its algorithm helps solve.

Navigation apps
Search engines
Streaming platforms
Online stores

Problems solved:

Recommending entertainment content
Finding information quickly
Suggesting products for customers
Calculating the fastest travel route

Chapter 1 Quiz

1. What is an algorithm?

A. A type of computer screen
B. A step-by-step set of instructions used to solve a problem
C. A type of internet connection
D. A computer storage device

2. Why do computers rely on algorithms?

A. Because computers can think independently
B. Because computers follow precise instructions to perform tasks
C. Because computers can guess answers
D. Because computers make emotional decisions

3. Which of the following technologies uses algorithms to rank information?

A. A calculator
B. A flashlight
C. A search engine
D. A keyboard

4. What type of system uses algorithms to suggest movies or music based on user behavior?

A. Navigation systems
B. Recommendation systems
C. Weather systems
D. File storage systems

5. Why is algorithmic thinking useful?

A. It helps people break problems into clear steps
B. It removes the need for computers
C. It replaces human decision making
D. It eliminates data processing

Quiz Answer Key

1. B — A step-by-step set of instructions used to solve a problem
2. B — Computers follow precise instructions to perform tasks
3. C — A search engine
4. B — Recommendation systems
5. A — It helps people break problems into clear steps

Chapter 2: What Is an Algorithm?

Algorithms are one of the most important concepts in computer science and modern technology. Every computer program, mobile application, and digital system depends on algorithms to perform tasks and solve problems. Although the word may sound technical, the idea behind an algorithm is simple. An algorithm is a clearly defined set of steps designed to accomplish a specific task or solve a particular problem.

In everyday life, people follow step-by-step instructions frequently. For example, following directions to a destination, preparing a recipe, or assembling furniture all involve a sequence of ordered steps. Each step must be completed in the correct order for the task to succeed. In the same way, computers rely on structured instructions that guide them through calculations and decision-making processes. These instructions form algorithms that allow machines to operate effectively.

Computers cannot make assumptions or interpret vague instructions. Unlike humans, computers require instructions that are precise and unambiguous. Every step of an algorithm must clearly specify what action the computer should take. When a programmer designs an algorithm, they must carefully define how the computer receives information, how it processes that information, and what result it should produce.

An algorithm always begins with input. Input is the information or data that a system receives in order to begin solving a problem. Input might come from a user typing on a keyboard, clicking a button, speaking into a microphone, or providing data through a sensor. Once the computer receives the input, the algorithm processes that information by performing calculations, comparisons, or logical decisions. The final result produced by the algorithm is called the output.

Consider a simple example involving a calculator application. When a user enters two numbers and selects an operation such as addition, the calculator receives the numbers as input. The algorithm then performs the mathematical operation according to the rules defined in the program. After completing the calculation, the computer displays the result as output. Although the process appears simple, it still relies on a defined sequence of algorithmic steps.

Algorithms can be used to solve a wide range of problems, from simple tasks to extremely complex challenges. Some algorithms sort information into a particular order, such as arranging numbers from smallest to largest. Other algorithms search through large collections of data in order to find specific information. More advanced algorithms analyze patterns, recognize images, or translate languages.

In modern computing systems, algorithms often operate on enormous amounts of data. For example, search engines analyze billions of web pages in order to provide relevant search results. To perform this task efficiently, the system relies on carefully designed algorithms that organize and rank information according to various factors. Without efficient algorithms, it would take an impractical amount of time to locate useful information within such large datasets.

Artificial intelligence systems also depend heavily on algorithms. In AI applications, algorithms analyze patterns within large datasets in order to learn relationships and make predictions. For example, a language translation system studies large collections of sentences written in different languages. By analyzing these examples, the algorithm learns patterns that help it generate translations for new sentences. While the system may appear to understand language, it is actually applying mathematical procedures that identify patterns within data.

One important characteristic of algorithms is that they must be reliable. When an algorithm receives the same input under the same conditions, it should consistently produce the same output. This consistency allows computer systems to perform tasks accurately and predictably. Engineers carefully test algorithms to ensure that they function correctly under a variety of conditions.

Efficiency is another important property of algorithms. Some algorithms can solve problems quickly, while others may require significantly more time or computing resources. When designing algorithms, computer scientists often compare different approaches to determine which one performs the task most efficiently. Efficient algorithms allow systems to process information faster and use fewer resources, which is especially important when working with large datasets.

Algorithms can be written in many different programming languages, but the underlying logic remains the same. Programmers may express algorithms using code, diagrams, or step-by-step descriptions that outline the process clearly. Regardless of how the instructions are written, the goal of the algorithm is to guide the computer through a structured sequence of operations that produces a correct result.

The concept of algorithms did not begin with modern computers. Mathematical procedures resembling algorithms have existed for thousands of years. Ancient mathematicians developed step-by-step methods for performing calculations such as multiplication and division. These procedures helped ensure that complex mathematical problems could be solved consistently. Over time, these methods evolved into the algorithmic principles used in modern computing.

Today, algorithms form the foundation of nearly every digital system. From the smallest mobile applications to the largest global networks, algorithms provide the logical framework that allows computers to perform useful tasks. They enable systems to process information, solve problems, and support technologies that influence daily life.

Learning about algorithms helps students understand how computers operate and how digital systems make decisions. Instead of viewing technology as a mysterious or magical tool, students can begin to see the logical processes that drive modern computing. This understanding encourages critical thinking and provides a foundation for exploring more advanced topics such as programming, data analysis, and artificial intelligence.

As technology continues to evolve, algorithms will remain central to the development of new systems and innovations. By understanding the principles behind algorithms, students gain valuable insight into the logic that powers modern technology and prepares them to participate in a world increasingly shaped by digital systems.

Chapter 2 Summary

Chapter 2 explained the fundamental concept of algorithms and their role in computing systems. An algorithm is a clearly defined sequence of steps used to solve a problem or perform a task. These instructions guide computers through processes that transform input data into meaningful output. Because computers cannot interpret vague or incomplete instructions, algorithms must be precise, logical, and organized.

The chapter described how algorithms begin with input, which is the data or information provided to a system. This input is processed through a sequence of steps that involve calculations, comparisons, or logical decisions. After these steps are completed, the system produces an output, which is the final result of the algorithm. This structure of input, processing, and output forms the foundation of most computing operations.

Examples of algorithms appear in many digital technologies. Calculator applications use algorithms to perform mathematical operations. Search engines rely on algorithms to locate and rank information from billions of websites. Artificial intelligence systems apply algorithms to analyze data patterns and generate predictions or recommendations.

Another important idea introduced in the chapter is the importance of reliability and efficiency. Reliable algorithms consistently produce the same correct output when given the same input. Efficient algorithms are designed to solve problems using the least amount of time and computational resources possible. Engineers and computer scientists often compare multiple algorithms to determine which approach performs a task most effectively.

The chapter also explained that algorithmic thinking is a valuable skill. This approach involves breaking complex problems into smaller steps that can be solved in sequence. Algorithmic thinking helps people design solutions logically and understand how digital systems operate. By learning how algorithms work, students gain insight into the logic that powers modern technology and develop the ability to think critically about the systems they use every day.

Reflection Questions

1. Why must algorithms provide clear and precise instructions for computers?
2. How does the structure of input, processing, and output help computers solve problems?
3. Think about a digital tool you use regularly. What type of input does the system receive and what output does it produce?
4. Why is efficiency important when designing algorithms?
5. How can learning algorithmic thinking help people solve problems in everyday life?

Worksheet: Understanding Algorithm Processes

Part A: Key Concepts

Write a short explanation for each term using your own words.

1. Algorithm
2. Input
3. Output
4. Processing
5. Efficiency

Part B: Algorithm Sequence

Below is an example situation. Arrange the steps in logical order.

A computer program calculates the average score of a student.

Steps (not in order):

Display the final average score
Add the scores together
Divide the total by the number of scores
Receive the list of scores from the user

Write the correct order of the steps:

Step 1
Step 2
Step 3
Step 4

Part C: Identifying Inputs and Outputs

Read the following situations and identify the input and output.

1. A calculator adds two numbers entered by a user.
   Input:
   Output:
2. A navigation app calculates the fastest route to a destination.
   Input:
   Output:
3. A search engine returns results for a question typed by a user.
   Input:
   Output:

Chapter 2 Quiz

1. What is the primary purpose of an algorithm?

A. To store computer hardware
B. To provide step-by-step instructions for solving a problem
C. To increase internet speed
D. To display images on a screen

2. What term describes the data that is provided to a computer system at the beginning of a process?

A. Output
B. Input
C. Calculation
D. Instruction

3. What is the result produced after a computer processes information through an algorithm?

A. Input
B. Process
C. Output
D. Storage

4. Why are efficient algorithms important?

A. They reduce the need for electricity
B. They solve problems using fewer resources and less time
C. They remove the need for programming
D. They allow computers to operate without instructions

5. What type of thinking involves breaking large problems into smaller steps?

A. Emotional thinking
B. Random thinking
C. Algorithmic thinking
D. Creative thinking

Quiz Answer Key

1. B — To provide step-by-step instructions for solving a problem
2. B — Input
3. C — Output
4. B — They solve problems using fewer resources and less time
5. C — Algorithmic thinking

Chapter 3: The History of Algorithms

The concept of algorithms did not begin with modern computers. Long before digital technology existed, humans developed step-by-step methods for solving mathematical and logical problems. These early procedures allowed people to perform calculations consistently and accurately. Over time, these systematic methods evolved into the algorithms that now power modern computing systems. Understanding the history of algorithms helps reveal how human problem-solving techniques gradually transformed into the structured instructions that guide today's digital technology.

The word "algorithm" itself has historical origins that date back more than a thousand years. The term is derived from the name of a Persian mathematician named Muhammad ibn Musa al-Khwarizmi, who lived during the ninth century. Al-Khwarizmi wrote influential mathematical texts that described systematic methods for solving arithmetic problems. His work introduced step-by-step procedures for performing calculations such as addition, subtraction, multiplication, and division. When his writings were translated into Latin centuries later, his name became associated with these procedural methods. Over time, the term evolved into the word "algorithm," which now refers broadly to any structured process used to solve a problem.

Even earlier civilizations developed algorithm-like procedures for solving mathematical challenges. Ancient Babylonian and Egyptian mathematicians created methods for performing calculations related to trade, construction, and astronomy. These early societies relied on organized steps to ensure that measurements and financial calculations were accurate. Although these procedures were not called algorithms at the time, they followed the same logical principles that define modern algorithmic thinking.

Ancient Greek mathematicians also contributed important ideas to the development of algorithms. One of the most well-known examples is the Euclidean algorithm, a method described by the Greek mathematician Euclid around 300 BCE. This procedure provides a systematic way to determine the greatest common divisor of two numbers. The Euclidean algorithm remains one of the oldest algorithms still studied and used today. Its continued relevance demonstrates how powerful and enduring well-designed problem-solving methods can be.

As mathematics continued to evolve, scholars across different cultures developed increasingly sophisticated methods for solving problems. During the medieval period, mathematicians in the Islamic world preserved and expanded many ancient mathematical ideas. Their work played an essential role in transmitting mathematical knowledge to Europe. Scholars translated important texts, developed new calculation methods, and improved numerical systems that made arithmetic more practical and efficient.

One major development during this period was the widespread adoption of the Hindu-Arabic numeral system, which introduced the digits 0 through 9 and the concept of positional value. This numerical system made calculations much easier than earlier Roman numeral methods. The improved efficiency of these calculations allowed more complex algorithms to be developed and applied in areas such as commerce, navigation, and engineering.

During the Renaissance and early modern periods, advances in mathematics and science led to further developments in algorithmic thinking. Mathematicians and scientists sought systematic ways to describe natural phenomena and solve increasingly complex problems. The development of algebra and calculus provided powerful mathematical tools that allowed researchers to model patterns, motion, and change. Many of these mathematical methods relied on structured sequences of steps similar to algorithms.

The Industrial Revolution brought another important shift in the evolution of algorithms. As machines became more common in manufacturing and engineering, scientists began to explore ways of automating calculations. Mechanical devices were developed to assist with arithmetic operations and data processing. Although these early machines were limited compared to modern computers, they demonstrated that machines could follow systematic procedures to perform useful tasks.

In the nineteenth century, an important milestone occurred when mathematician Charles Babbage designed a conceptual mechanical computer known as the Analytical Engine. Babbage envisioned a machine capable of performing complex calculations automatically by following programmed instructions. Although the machine was never fully completed during his lifetime, his ideas laid the groundwork for future computing systems. Ada Lovelace, who worked closely with Babbage, wrote detailed descriptions of how the Analytical Engine could follow instructions to perform calculations. Her writings are often considered among the first examples of computer programming concepts.

The twentieth century marked a turning point in the development of algorithms. Advances in mathematics and engineering led to the creation of electronic computers capable of executing instructions at high speed. One of the most influential thinkers of this era was British mathematician Alan Turing. Turing developed a theoretical model known as the Turing machine, which demonstrated how a machine could follow a sequence of logical instructions to solve mathematical problems. His work helped establish the theoretical foundation of computer science and showed that complex computations could be performed through systematic algorithms.

As electronic computers became more powerful during the mid-twentieth century, researchers began developing increasingly sophisticated algorithms for solving scientific and engineering problems. Early computers were used for tasks such as weather prediction, military calculations, and space exploration. The success of these systems demonstrated the practical importance of well-designed algorithms in solving complex real-world challenges.

During the late twentieth century, the rapid growth of the internet and digital communication networks expanded the role of algorithms even further. Search engines, online databases, and communication systems relied on algorithms to organize and retrieve information efficiently. New types of algorithms were developed to manage large datasets, optimize network performance, and support digital commerce.

In the twenty-first century, algorithms have become central to artificial intelligence and data science. Machine learning algorithms analyze enormous collections of data in order to detect patterns and make predictions. These algorithms power technologies such as voice recognition, image classification, language translation, and recommendation systems. Although the scale and complexity of modern algorithms have grown dramatically, the underlying principle remains the same: solving problems through clearly defined steps.

The history of algorithms demonstrates that structured problem solving has been an essential part of human progress for thousands of years. From ancient mathematical procedures to modern artificial intelligence systems, algorithms have continually evolved as tools for understanding and managing complex information. By studying the historical development of algorithms, students gain a deeper appreciation for how human creativity and logical thinking have shaped the digital technologies that influence the modern world.

Chapter 3 Summary

Chapter 3 explored the historical development of algorithms and how structured problem-solving methods evolved long before the invention of modern computers. Although algorithms are now closely associated with digital technology, the idea of solving problems through step-by-step procedures has existed for thousands of years. Early civilizations created systematic methods for performing calculations related to trade, construction, and astronomy. These procedures helped ensure accuracy and consistency when solving mathematical problems.

The chapter explained that the word "algorithm" comes from the name of the ninth-century Persian mathematician Muhammad ibn Musa al-Khwarizmi. His writings described clear procedures for performing arithmetic calculations. When his work was translated into Latin, his name became associated with these step-by-step calculation methods, eventually giving rise to the modern term "algorithm."

The chapter also introduced the contributions of ancient Greek mathematician Euclid, who developed the Euclidean algorithm around 300 BCE. This method for finding the greatest common divisor of two numbers is one of the oldest known algorithms still studied today. It demonstrates how logical procedures can remain useful across centuries of scientific development.

Throughout history, mathematicians across many cultures continued to refine algorithmic thinking. During the medieval period, scholars preserved and expanded earlier mathematical knowledge and introduced improved numerical systems, including the Hindu-Arabic numeral system. This system made calculations more efficient and allowed increasingly complex mathematical methods to be developed.

Later developments in science and engineering led to the creation of mechanical devices designed to assist with calculations. In the nineteenth century, Charles Babbage proposed the Analytical Engine, a conceptual mechanical computer capable of following programmed instructions. Ada Lovelace expanded on Babbage's ideas by describing how such machines could execute sequences of operations, an early form of computer programming.

In the twentieth century, mathematician Alan Turing helped establish the theoretical foundations of modern computer science. His concept of the Turing machine demonstrated how machines could solve problems by following precise logical instructions. As electronic computers developed, algorithms became essential for scientific research, engineering, and data processing.

Today algorithms power many modern technologies, including search engines, communication networks, and artificial intelligence systems. The chapter demonstrated that algorithms are not a recent invention but rather the result of centuries of human effort to develop reliable methods for solving problems. Understanding this historical development helps students appreciate how algorithmic thinking has shaped both mathematics and modern digital technology.

Reflection Questions

1. Why is it important to understand that algorithms existed long before modern computers?
2. How did early civilizations use step-by-step procedures to solve practical problems?
3. Why is the work of al-Khwarizmi considered important in the history of algorithms?
4. What does the continued use of the Euclidean algorithm show about well-designed problem-solving methods?
5. How did early ideas about mechanical computing machines contribute to the development of modern algorithms?

Worksheet: Exploring the History of Algorithms

Part A: Key Figures in Algorithm History

Write a short explanation describing the contribution of each historical figure.

1. Muhammad ibn Musa al-Khwarizmi
2. Euclid
3. Charles Babbage
4. Ada Lovelace
5. Alan Turing

Part B: Timeline of Algorithm Development

Place the following developments in the correct historical order.

Development of electronic computers
Euclid describes the Euclidean algorithm
Al-Khwarizmi writes mathematical procedures
Charles Babbage proposes the Analytical Engine

Write the correct order from earliest to most recent.

1.
2.
3.
4.

Part C: Understanding Algorithm Evolution

Explain in a short paragraph how algorithmic thinking evolved from ancient mathematical procedures to modern computing systems.

Chapter 3 Quiz

1. The word "algorithm" is derived from the name of which historical mathematician?

A. Isaac Newton
B. Muhammad ibn Musa al-Khwarizmi
C. Galileo Galilei
D. Nikola Tesla

2. Which ancient mathematician developed an early algorithm for finding the greatest common divisor of two numbers?

A. Aristotle
B. Euclid
C. Pythagoras
D. Archimedes

3. What was the Analytical Engine designed by Charles Babbage intended to do?

A. Perform automated calculations using programmed instructions
B. Store digital photographs
C. Control communication networks
D. Display written documents

4. Who is often recognized for writing one of the earliest descriptions of computer programming concepts?

A. Ada Lovelace
B. Marie Curie
C. Grace Hopper
D. Katherine Johnson

5. What concept did Alan Turing introduce that helped establish the theoretical foundations of computing?

A. Artificial neural networks
B. The Turing machine
C. Cloud computing
D. Digital photography

Chapter 4: Bits, Logic, and Digital Instructions

Modern computers are capable of performing extraordinary tasks. They can analyze large datasets, power global communication networks, translate languages, and support scientific discoveries. Although these systems may appear highly complex, they are built upon a surprisingly simple foundation. At the most fundamental level, computers operate using small units of information called bits and follow logical instructions that guide every operation they perform. Understanding how bits and logic work together provides insight into how computers interpret instructions and execute algorithms.

A bit is the smallest unit of digital information. The word "bit" is short for "binary digit," which reflects the two possible values a bit can represent. A bit can hold a value of either 0 or 1. These two states correspond to physical electrical signals inside a computer's hardware. In many electronic circuits, the value 1 represents the presence of an electrical signal, while the value 0 represents the absence of that signal. By using combinations of these two states, computers can represent numbers, letters, images, and many other forms of information.

Although a single bit can represent only two possible values, groups of bits can represent far more complex information. For example, eight bits combined together form a unit called a byte. A byte can represent many different numerical values, which allows computers to store characters, symbols, and instructions. Larger collections of bits allow computers to represent more complicated forms of data such as images, sound recordings, and video files. In this way, the entire digital world is built from combinations of simple binary signals.

The use of binary numbers allows computers to operate reliably using electronic circuits. Binary representation simplifies the design of computer hardware because circuits can easily distinguish between two electrical states. This design reduces the likelihood of errors and makes digital systems more stable. By representing information in binary form, computers can process and store data efficiently using electronic components that switch between two states.

Bits by themselves do not perform actions. Instead, they form the building blocks that allow computers to represent data and instructions. When programmers write software, their instructions are eventually translated into binary code that the computer's hardware can interpret. This binary code tells the computer which operations to perform and in what order those operations should occur. The processor inside the computer reads these instructions and executes them one step at a time.

In order to perform meaningful tasks, computers rely on logical operations. Logic provides a system of rules that determines how decisions are made within a program. These logical rules allow computers to compare values, evaluate conditions, and determine which actions should occur next. Logic is essential because many computational problems involve choices that depend on specific conditions.

One of the most important systems used in computing is Boolean logic. Boolean logic is a form of algebra developed by mathematician George Boole in the nineteenth century. It describes how logical statements can be combined and evaluated using operators such as AND, OR, and NOT. These logical operators allow computers to determine whether certain conditions are true or false. Because digital circuits operate using binary states, Boolean logic fits naturally with computer hardware.

Logical operations occur constantly inside modern computing systems. For example, a computer program might evaluate whether a number is greater than another number. It may check whether a password entered by a user matches stored information. It may also determine whether a particular condition has been satisfied before continuing with the next step of a process. Each of these decisions relies on logical comparisons that produce either a true or false result.

When computers execute algorithms, they combine binary data with logical operations to perform structured sequences of instructions. The processor reads an instruction from memory, interprets the operation described by the instruction, and performs the required calculation or comparison. After completing one instruction, the processor moves to the next instruction in the sequence. This cycle continues repeatedly as the computer executes the algorithm.

The relationship between bits and logic forms the foundation of all digital instructions. Each instruction that a computer executes is represented as a pattern of bits. These patterns correspond to specific operations that the processor understands. Some instructions may perform arithmetic calculations such as addition or subtraction. Others may move data between memory locations or evaluate logical conditions. Regardless of the specific task, each instruction ultimately depends on the binary representation of information.

Modern computers perform these operations at extraordinary speeds. A typical processor can execute billions of instructions every second. Despite this speed, the underlying process remains systematic and structured. The processor continuously reads instructions from memory, processes them according to logical rules, and produces results that may influence subsequent operations. This cycle of reading, processing, and executing instructions forms the basic operation of a computer.

Bits and logical operations also make it possible to store and manipulate different types of data. Text, images, sound, and video are all represented using binary numbers. For example, letters and characters are assigned numerical codes that correspond to binary patterns. Images are represented as collections of pixels, each described by numerical values that indicate color and brightness. Audio recordings are stored as sequences of numbers that represent variations in sound waves. In every case, the computer uses bits to represent information and logical instructions to process it.

In addition to supporting data representation, logic plays a crucial role in decision-making processes within software. Programs often include conditional instructions that determine how the system responds to different situations. For example, a program may check whether a file exists before attempting to open it. A navigation system may determine whether traffic conditions require a change in route. A security system may verify whether login credentials match stored records. These decisions rely on logical comparisons that guide the behavior of the system.

Digital circuits inside computer processors are specifically designed to perform logical operations efficiently. Engineers construct circuits called logic gates that implement Boolean operations such as AND, OR, and NOT. These gates combine electrical signals in ways that produce predictable outcomes based on logical rules. By connecting many logic gates together, engineers create complex circuits capable of performing sophisticated computations. These circuits form the foundation of modern processors and computing devices.

Although computers appear capable of intelligent behavior, their operation ultimately depends on the interaction between binary data and logical instructions. Every application, from simple calculators to advanced artificial intelligence systems, relies on these fundamental principles. Algorithms describe the sequence of steps required to solve a problem, but those steps must be executed using binary representations and logical operations inside the hardware.

Understanding bits and logic helps students recognize that computers operate through structured systems rather than independent thought. Machines do not interpret meaning or make decisions in the way humans do. Instead, they follow logical instructions that process data in precise ways. These instructions allow computers to perform useful tasks quickly and accurately, but the underlying mechanism remains a series of carefully defined operations.

As digital technology continues to advance, the importance of binary representation and logical reasoning remains unchanged. New programming languages, powerful processors, and sophisticated software systems all rely on the same fundamental principles established in the early days of computing. By learning how bits and logic form the basis of digital instructions, students gain a deeper understanding of how computers execute algorithms and support the technologies that shape modern life.

The concepts explored in this chapter form an essential part of the foundation of computer science. Bits provide the smallest units of information, while logic determines how that information is processed and interpreted. Together, these elements create the framework that allows computers to execute instructions, analyze data, and support the complex digital systems used throughout the world today.

Chapter 4 Summary

Chapter 4 explained the foundational relationship between bits, logic, and digital instructions in modern computing systems. Although computers appear capable of performing complex tasks, their operation is built upon simple digital principles. The smallest unit of digital information is the bit, which represents one of two possible values: 0 or 1. These values correspond to electrical states inside computer circuits and form the basis of binary representation.

By combining bits into larger groups, computers are able to represent increasingly complex forms of information. Groups of eight bits form a byte, which can store characters, numbers, or other types of data. Larger collections of bits allow computers to represent images, sound, video, and many other forms of digital content. In this way, all digital information is ultimately built from combinations of binary signals.

The chapter also introduced the concept of logic in computing. Logic provides the rules that allow computers to make decisions while executing instructions. Boolean logic, developed by mathematician George Boole, describes how logical operations such as AND, OR, and NOT allow computers to evaluate conditions. These logical operations produce true or false outcomes that guide how a program continues executing instructions.

Computers combine binary data and logical operations in order to execute algorithms. Each instruction processed by the computer is represented as a pattern of bits. The processor reads these instructions, interprets them according to logical rules, and performs the required calculations or comparisons. This process occurs repeatedly as the computer executes software programs.

The chapter also discussed how digital circuits called logic gates perform logical operations within computer hardware. These circuits combine electrical signals in ways that follow Boolean logic, allowing computers to perform complex calculations at high speed. By connecting large numbers of logic gates together, engineers create processors capable of executing billions of instructions each second.

Understanding bits and logic helps students recognize how computers process information and follow instructions. Rather than thinking independently, computers operate through precise sequences of logical operations applied to binary data. These foundational concepts support everything from simple applications to advanced artificial intelligence systems.

Reflection Questions

1. Why do computers use binary numbers instead of more complex numerical systems?
2. How do bits combine to represent different types of digital information such as text, images, or sound?
3. Why is logic necessary for computers to make decisions during program execution?
4. How do logic gates help computers perform calculations and comparisons?
5. Why is it important for students to understand the relationship between bits, logic, and algorithms?

Worksheet: Bits and Logic in Computing

Part A: Key Concepts

Write a short explanation for each term.

1. Bit
2. Byte
3. Binary system
4. Boolean logic
5. Logic gate

Part B: Binary Understanding

Answer the following questions.

1. What two values can a bit represent?
2. How many bits are in one byte?
3. Why is binary representation useful for electronic circuits?

Part C: Logic in Action

Describe how logic might be used in the following situations.

1. A computer checks whether a password entered by a user matches a stored password.
2. A navigation system determines whether traffic conditions require a new route.
3. A website verifies whether a user has entered valid login information.

Chapter 4 Quiz

1. What is the smallest unit of digital information in computing?

A. Byte
B. Bit
C. File
D. Program

2. What two values can a bit represent?

A. 1 and 2
B. 0 and 2
C. 0 and 1
D. 1 and 10

3. What term describes a group of eight bits?

A. Byte
B. Block
C. Node
D. Segment

4. Which system of logic is commonly used in computing to evaluate true or false conditions?

A. Geometric logic
B. Boolean logic
C. Linear logic
D. Chemical logic

5. What electronic component performs logical operations inside computer circuits?

A. Logic gate
B. Monitor
C. Hard drive
D. Network cable

Quiz Answer Key

1. B — Bit
2. C — 0 and 1
3. A — Byte
4. B — Boolean logic
5. A — Logic gate

Chapter 5: How Computers Execute Algorithms

Computers are powerful machines capable of performing billions of operations every second, yet the way they carry out tasks follows a structured and orderly process. When a computer runs a program, it is executing a sequence of instructions that have been carefully written by programmers. These instructions form algorithms that guide the computer through problem-solving procedures. Understanding how computers execute algorithms helps reveal how software systems function and how machines process information in a reliable and predictable way.

Every computer contains a central component responsible for executing instructions. This component is known as the central processing unit, or CPU. The CPU acts as the control center of the computer, interpreting and carrying out the instructions that make up a program. When software is launched, the instructions that define the program are loaded into the computer's memory so the CPU can access them. The processor then begins executing those instructions step by step according to the structure defined by the algorithm.

The execution of algorithms follows a repeating cycle known as the instruction cycle. During this cycle, the CPU retrieves an instruction from memory, interprets what the instruction requires, and performs the appropriate operation. After completing the instruction, the CPU moves to the next instruction in the sequence and repeats the process. This continuous cycle allows the computer to execute complex programs by performing many small operations in rapid succession.

The first stage of the instruction cycle is called the fetch phase. In this stage, the CPU retrieves the next instruction from the computer's memory. Each instruction is stored in memory as a pattern of binary digits that represent a specific operation. The CPU reads this instruction and temporarily stores it in a special location within the processor so it can be interpreted.

After fetching the instruction, the processor enters the decode phase. During this stage, the CPU analyzes the binary instruction and determines what action must be performed. Different patterns of bits correspond to different operations, such as performing a calculation, moving data from one location to another, or comparing two values. The decoding process translates the binary pattern into a meaningful action that the processor can carry out.

Once the instruction has been decoded, the CPU moves to the execute phase. During this stage, the processor performs the operation specified by the instruction. This operation may involve performing arithmetic calculations, evaluating logical conditions, or transferring data between memory locations. Some instructions may also cause the computer to interact with input or output devices, such as displaying information on a screen or reading data from a keyboard.

After the execution stage is completed, the processor prepares to repeat the cycle by fetching the next instruction. This continuous sequence of fetching, decoding, and executing instructions allows computers to perform extremely complex operations. Even though a program may appear to perform many tasks simultaneously, the CPU is actually executing instructions one after another at extremely high speeds.

The instructions that a computer executes are part of a program written in a programming language. Programming languages allow developers to describe algorithms using human-readable syntax. Languages such as Python, Java, and C++ provide tools that help programmers organize instructions, perform calculations, and manage data. However, computers cannot directly understand these languages. Before a program can be executed, it must be translated into machine code.

Machine code is the lowest-level language that a computer can understand. It consists entirely of binary instructions that correspond directly to operations the processor can perform. Special programs called compilers or interpreters translate high-level programming languages into machine code. This translation ensures that the instructions written by programmers can be executed by the computer's hardware.

Memory plays a crucial role in the execution of algorithms. When a program runs, both the instructions and the data used by the program are stored in memory. The CPU constantly reads from and writes to memory as it executes instructions. Some data may be stored temporarily during calculations, while other information may be stored more permanently for later use. Efficient use of memory allows algorithms to process large amounts of information without slowing down the system.

In addition to the CPU and memory, computers rely on input and output systems to interact with users and other devices. Input devices allow the computer to receive information from the outside world. Examples include keyboards, microphones, sensors, and touchscreens. Output devices allow the computer to present results to users, such as displaying information on a monitor or producing sound through speakers. Algorithms often include instructions that handle input and output operations, enabling computers to respond to user requests and provide useful feedback.

Programs often include control structures that determine how algorithms proceed through instructions. Control structures allow programs to repeat certain steps or make decisions based on specific conditions. For example, a program might repeat a calculation several times until a certain result is reached. In other situations, the program may choose between different instructions depending on whether a condition is true or false. These structures allow algorithms to adapt to different situations and handle complex tasks more effectively.

Loops are one type of control structure commonly used in algorithms. A loop allows a computer to repeat a set of instructions multiple times. This capability is useful when performing tasks that require repetitive processing, such as analyzing each item in a large dataset. By repeating instructions efficiently, loops allow algorithms to perform large-scale computations while minimizing the amount of code required.

Conditional statements represent another important control structure. These statements allow programs to evaluate conditions and choose different actions depending on the result. For example, a program may check whether a user has entered valid login credentials. If the credentials are correct, the program allows access to the system. If the credentials are incorrect, the program displays an error message and requests another attempt. Conditional logic enables algorithms to respond dynamically to different inputs.

The ability to combine loops, conditional statements, and structured instructions allows algorithms to perform increasingly complex operations. Simple algorithms may perform straightforward tasks such as adding numbers or sorting lists. More advanced algorithms may analyze large datasets, simulate scientific models, or support artificial intelligence systems.

Regardless of complexity, every algorithm is ultimately executed through the same basic instruction cycle performed by the CPU.

Modern processors perform these operations at remarkable speeds. A single processor may execute billions of instructions each second. Many computers also contain multiple processor cores that allow several instructions to be processed simultaneously. This capability allows modern systems to perform multiple tasks at once, such as running applications, processing network communications, and displaying graphics.

Despite the impressive capabilities of modern computing systems, the underlying process of executing algorithms remains systematic and structured. Each program is broken into small instructions that the processor executes step by step. These instructions follow logical rules and operate on binary data stored in memory. The speed and efficiency of this process allow computers to solve problems that would be extremely difficult for humans to calculate manually.

Understanding how computers execute algorithms helps students see the relationship between software and hardware. Programs written by developers become instructions that the computer's processor can interpret and execute. The processor follows these instructions through the instruction cycle, performing calculations, making comparisons, and producing results. Through this process, algorithms become the operational framework that allows computers to perform meaningful tasks.

As students learn more about computing systems, they begin to recognize that even the most advanced technologies rely on these fundamental processes. Whether supporting a simple application or powering complex artificial intelligence systems, computers execute algorithms by following precise sequences of instructions. This structured approach ensures that digital systems operate reliably and consistently, forming the foundation of modern computing.

Chapter 5 Summary

Chapter 5 explained how computers execute algorithms through a structured and repeating process. Although software programs may appear complex, computers perform tasks by following clear instructions step by step. These instructions are interpreted and executed by the central processing unit, commonly called the CPU. The CPU acts as the control center of the computer and is responsible for reading instructions, processing them, and carrying out the required operations.

The chapter introduced the instruction cycle, which describes the process the CPU follows when executing a program. This cycle consists of three main stages. First, the processor fetches an instruction from memory. Next, the processor decodes the instruction to determine the operation that must be performed. Finally, the processor executes the instruction by performing a calculation, comparison, or data transfer. This cycle repeats continuously as the computer processes instructions.

Programming languages allow developers to write algorithms using human-readable instructions. However, computers cannot directly understand these languages. Before a program can run, the instructions must be translated into machine code. Machine code consists of binary instructions that the processor can interpret and execute. Compilers and interpreters are special programs that convert human-readable code into machine code.

Memory also plays an essential role in algorithm execution. Both the instructions and the data used by a program are stored in memory while the program runs. The processor retrieves instructions from memory, processes data, and stores results back into memory. Efficient use of memory helps computers handle large amounts of information without slowing down performance.

The chapter also discussed control structures, which allow programs to repeat actions or make decisions. Loops allow instructions to be repeated multiple times, while conditional statements allow a program to choose between different actions depending on whether a condition is true or false. These structures enable algorithms to handle complex tasks and respond to different situations.

Understanding how computers execute algorithms helps students see how software and hardware work together. Programs written by developers become instructions that processors execute through a structured process. By following this sequence of operations, computers are able to solve problems, process data, and power the digital systems used throughout modern society.

Reflection Questions

1. Why is the CPU considered the control center of a computer?
2. How does the instruction cycle help computers execute algorithms efficiently?
3. Why must programming languages be translated into machine code before a computer can run a program?
4. How do loops and conditional statements allow algorithms to solve more complex problems?
5. Why is memory important when a computer executes instructions?

Worksheet: Understanding Algorithm Execution

Part A: Key Terms

Write a short explanation for each term.

1. Central Processing Unit (CPU)
2. Instruction cycle
3. Machine code

4. Compiler or interpreter
5. Control structure

Part B: Instruction Cycle

Place the following stages of the instruction cycle in the correct order.

Execute the instruction
Fetch the instruction from memory
Decode the instruction

Write the correct sequence:

Step 1
Step 2
Step 3

Part C: Identifying Computer Components

Explain the role of each component when executing algorithms.

1. CPU
2. Memory
3. Input devices
4. Output devices

Chapter 5 Quiz

1. Which component of a computer executes instructions in a program?

A. Monitor
B. CPU
C. Keyboard
D. Printer

2. What is the first stage of the instruction cycle?

A. Decode
B. Execute

C. Fetch
D. Store

3. What type of code can a computer processor directly understand?

A. Machine code
B. Text code
C. Web code
D. Image code

4. What program translates human-readable programming languages into machine code?

A. Browser
B. Compiler or interpreter
C. Spreadsheet
D. Database

5. What type of control structure allows a program to repeat instructions multiple times?

A. Loop
B. Variable
C. Function
D. Database

Quiz Answer Key

1. B — CPU
2. C — Fetch
3. A — Machine code
4. B — Compiler or interpreter
5. A — Loop

Chapter 6: Breaking Problems into Steps

One of the most important skills in computer science is the ability to break complex problems into smaller, manageable parts. Computers are powerful machines, but they rely on clear and structured instructions in order to perform useful tasks. When programmers design algorithms, they must carefully analyze a problem and determine the sequence of steps required to solve it. This process of dividing a problem into smaller pieces is often called decomposition, and it forms the foundation of algorithmic thinking.

Many problems in everyday life appear complicated at first glance. However, when those problems are examined carefully, they can often be solved by completing a series of smaller tasks in the correct order. Humans naturally use this approach in many situations. For example, preparing a meal involves gathering ingredients, measuring quantities, following cooking steps, and serving the finished dish. Each action builds upon the previous step until the final outcome is achieved. Computers rely on a similar process when executing algorithms.

When designing an algorithm, the first step is to clearly understand the problem that needs to be solved. Programmers must determine what information will be required, what actions must occur, and what result should be produced. This process involves identifying the input that the system will receive and the output that it should generate. By defining these elements clearly, developers can begin designing the sequence of steps needed to transform the input into the desired output.

Once the problem is understood, the next step is to divide the task into smaller operations. These smaller operations are easier to manage and test individually. Each step in the algorithm should perform a specific action that contributes to the overall solution. By organizing these steps logically, programmers create a structured pathway that the computer can follow.

Breaking problems into smaller steps helps reduce complexity. Large problems can often feel overwhelming if they are approached all at once. By focusing on one small task at a time, programmers can gradually construct a complete solution. This method also allows developers to identify potential errors more easily because each step can be tested independently before it becomes part of a larger system.

In computer science, this process of dividing problems into smaller pieces is often referred to as modular design. A module is a small section of a program that performs a specific task. Instead of writing one large block of instructions, programmers create smaller modules that work together to solve the overall problem. Each module can be developed, tested, and improved separately, making the entire system easier to understand and maintain.

For example, imagine designing a program that calculates the average score of a group of students. Instead of writing one large set of instructions, the programmer might divide the task into several smaller steps. One part of the program collects the student scores. Another part calculates the total sum of the scores. A third part divides the total by the number of students to produce the average. By separating the problem into modules, the program becomes easier to design and troubleshoot.

Another important concept when breaking problems into steps is sequencing. Sequencing refers to the order in which instructions are executed. For an algorithm to work correctly, the steps must occur in the correct sequence. If instructions are performed out of order, the program may produce incorrect results or fail to operate entirely. Careful sequencing ensures that each step builds logically upon the previous step.

In addition to sequencing, algorithms often include repetition. Some tasks require the same operation to be performed multiple times. For example, a program analyzing a list of numbers may need to examine each number individually. Rather than writing separate instructions for every item, programmers use loops that repeat a set of instructions until all items have been processed. Repetition allows algorithms to handle large datasets efficiently.

Decision making is another important element of algorithm design. Many problems require the system to choose between different actions depending on certain conditions. For example, a program might need to determine whether a number is positive or negative, or whether a user has entered valid login credentials. Conditional instructions allow algorithms to evaluate conditions and respond accordingly. This capability enables programs to adapt to different inputs and situations.

When programmers design algorithms, they often create diagrams or written descriptions that outline the steps of the solution before writing actual code. One common tool used in algorithm design is the flowchart. A flowchart visually represents the sequence of operations in an algorithm. Each step is shown as a symbol connected by arrows that indicate the flow of the process. Flowcharts help programmers visualize how instructions move through the algorithm and how decisions affect the path of execution.

Another common method for describing algorithms is pseudocode. Pseudocode is a simplified form of writing that resembles programming language but is easier to read and understand. It allows programmers to describe the logic of an algorithm without worrying about the exact syntax of a specific programming language. By writing pseudocode first, developers can focus on the logical structure of the solution before translating it into actual code.

Breaking problems into steps is also an essential skill for debugging programs. Debugging is the process of identifying and correcting errors in a program. When an algorithm is organized into smaller components, it becomes easier to locate the source of a problem. Developers can test individual steps or modules to determine where an error is occurring and then correct the issue without affecting the entire system.

Algorithmic thinking extends beyond computer programming. The ability to analyze problems, divide them into smaller tasks, and solve them systematically is a valuable skill in many fields. Engineers, scientists, doctors, and business leaders all rely on structured problem-solving methods when addressing complex challenges. By learning algorithmic thinking, students develop logical reasoning skills that can be applied in many different areas of study and professional practice.

In modern computing systems, the ability to break problems into steps is especially important because software applications often involve thousands or even millions of instructions. Without careful organization, such systems would be difficult to develop or maintain. By designing algorithms with clear structure and modular components, developers create programs that are easier to understand, update, and expand.

Large technology systems used in industries such as transportation, healthcare, finance, and communication all depend on well-structured algorithms. For example, airline scheduling systems must coordinate thousands of flights, passengers, and crew members. Medical software must analyze patient data and assist healthcare professionals in making informed decisions. Financial systems must process transactions quickly and securely. In each case, complex problems are solved by dividing tasks into smaller steps and organizing them into reliable algorithms.

As students learn more about algorithm design, they begin to see that even the most advanced technologies rely on simple logical principles. By carefully analyzing problems and organizing solutions into structured steps, programmers create algorithms that guide computers through complex tasks. This approach allows machines to process information efficiently and produce accurate results.

Breaking problems into steps is therefore a central idea in both computing and problem solving. It allows complex challenges to be approached systematically and makes it possible for computers to execute algorithms reliably. By mastering this skill, students gain a deeper understanding of how algorithms are designed and how computers transform instructions into meaningful outcomes in the digital world.

Chapter 6 Summary

Chapter 6 focused on one of the most important ideas in algorithm design: breaking complex problems into smaller, manageable steps. Computers cannot solve large problems all at once. Instead, programmers must analyze the problem carefully and divide it into a sequence of smaller operations that can be executed in an organized order. This process is often called decomposition and is a key part of algorithmic thinking.

The chapter explained that algorithm design begins by clearly understanding the problem to be solved. Programmers must identify the input that the system will receive and the output that the system should produce. Once these elements are defined, developers can begin constructing the sequence of steps required to transform the input into the desired result.

Dividing problems into smaller tasks helps reduce complexity and makes solutions easier to develop and test. Each step of an algorithm performs a specific function that contributes to the final outcome. When algorithms are organized into smaller modules, each module can be developed and tested independently. This modular design approach allows programmers to build reliable systems that are easier to maintain and improve.

The chapter also introduced the importance of sequencing, repetition, and decision-making in algorithms. Sequencing ensures that instructions occur in the correct order. Repetition allows a set of instructions to be repeated when tasks must be performed multiple times. Decision-making allows algorithms to respond differently depending on certain conditions. These elements allow algorithms to handle complex situations and adapt to different inputs.

Tools such as flowcharts and pseudocode help programmers visualize and design algorithms before writing computer code. Flowcharts represent the steps of an algorithm using visual symbols, while pseudocode describes the logical structure of a solution using simplified language. These tools help developers organize their ideas and detect potential errors early in the design process.

The chapter also emphasized that algorithmic thinking is useful beyond computer science. The ability to analyze problems, divide them into smaller tasks, and solve them logically is valuable in many fields, including science, engineering, medicine, and business. By developing these skills, students learn structured approaches to solving problems that can be applied in many areas of life.

Understanding how to break problems into steps helps students recognize that even complex technologies rely on simple logical processes. By organizing solutions carefully and designing clear instructions, programmers create algorithms that allow computers to process information efficiently and solve challenging problems.

Reflection Questions

1. Why is it important to divide complex problems into smaller steps when designing algorithms?
2. How does modular design make computer programs easier to understand and maintain?
3. Why must the steps of an algorithm be arranged in the correct sequence?
4. How do repetition and decision-making allow algorithms to solve more complex problems?
5. In what ways can algorithmic thinking help people solve problems outside of computer science?

Worksheet: Breaking Problems into Steps

Part A: Understanding Key Concepts

Write a short explanation for each term.

1. Decomposition
2. Modular design
3. Sequencing
4. Repetition
5. Decision-making

Part B: Organizing Algorithm Steps

Below are steps for calculating the average of three numbers. The steps are out of order.

Divide the total by three
Add the three numbers together
Display the average
Receive the three numbers as input

Write the correct sequence.

Step 1
Step 2
Step 3
Step 4

Part C: Designing an Everyday Algorithm

Choose one of the following tasks and describe the steps needed to complete it.

Making a sandwich
Preparing for school in the morning
Sending an email

Write the steps in order.

Step 1
Step 2
Step 3
Step 4
Step 5

Chapter 6 Quiz

1. What process involves dividing a complex problem into smaller tasks?

A. Compilation
B. Decomposition
C. Translation
D. Compression

2. What term describes organizing a program into smaller sections that perform specific tasks?

A. Modular design
B. Binary coding

C. Encryption
D. Networking

3. What concept ensures that instructions in an algorithm occur in the correct order?

A. Sequencing
B. Translation
C. Encoding
D. Storage

4. What structure allows a program to repeat a set of instructions multiple times?

A. Loop
B. Variable
C. Database
D. Display

5. What tool visually represents the steps of an algorithm using diagrams?

A. Flowchart
B. Spreadsheet
C. Database
D. Browser

Quiz Answer Key

1. B — Decomposition
2. A — Modular design
3. A — Sequencing
4. A — Loop
5. A — Flowchart

Chapter 7: Data and Algorithms — How Information Drives Decisions

Algorithms cannot function without information. Every algorithm depends on data in order to perform calculations, evaluate conditions, and produce meaningful results. In computing, data refers to any form of information that can be processed by a computer. This information may include numbers, words, images, sounds, or measurements collected from sensors and devices. Without data, algorithms would have nothing to analyze and no problems to solve.

In everyday life, humans constantly use information to make decisions. When deciding what clothes to wear, a person might consider the weather, the temperature, and the activities planned for the day. Each of these pieces of information helps guide the final choice. Computers operate in a similar way. Algorithms analyze data in order to determine what action should be taken or what result should be produced.

Before an algorithm can process data, that information must be represented in a format that computers can understand. As discussed in earlier chapters, computers store and process information using binary numbers composed of bits. These binary values allow computers to represent many different types of data. Letters and words can be represented through character encoding systems. Numbers can be stored in various numeric formats. Images and sound can be translated into digital signals that computers can process.

Once data is represented digitally, algorithms can manipulate it in many ways. Some algorithms perform calculations using numerical data, such as computing averages, totals, or measurements. Other algorithms analyze patterns in data, searching for relationships or trends. In modern computing systems, algorithms also sort, filter, and organize large collections of data so that information can be retrieved efficiently.

Sorting is one of the most common operations performed by algorithms. Sorting algorithms arrange data in a specific order, such as alphabetical order or numerical order. For example, a program might sort a list of student names alphabetically or arrange test scores from highest to lowest. Sorting helps make information easier to find and analyze. Many computer systems rely on sorting algorithms to manage large databases and digital records.

Searching is another essential function of algorithms. Searching algorithms locate specific information within a dataset. For example, when someone types a name into a search bar or looks up a contact in a phone list, a searching algorithm scans through the stored data to find the requested information. Efficient searching becomes increasingly important as the amount of stored data grows larger.

Algorithms also use data to make decisions. Conditional instructions allow programs to evaluate data and determine which action should be taken. For example, an online shopping system might check whether a product is in stock before allowing a purchase to proceed. A weather application might analyze temperature data to determine whether to display a heat advisory or a cold-weather alert. In each case, algorithms examine available data and follow logical rules to produce an outcome.

The relationship between data and algorithms becomes even more important in modern artificial intelligence systems. AI models rely on large datasets to learn patterns and improve their performance. Machine learning algorithms analyze enormous amounts of information in order to identify relationships that may not be immediately obvious to humans. For example, AI systems can analyze medical images to help detect diseases, or they can analyze traffic patterns to optimize transportation systems.

Data quality plays a crucial role in the effectiveness of algorithms. If the data used by an algorithm is incomplete, inaccurate, or biased, the results produced by the system may also be flawed. This concept is sometimes summarized by the phrase "garbage in, garbage out," which means that poor-quality data leads to poor-quality outcomes. Ensuring that data is accurate and reliable is therefore an important responsibility for developers and organizations that rely on algorithms.

Another important consideration when working with data is privacy and security. Many algorithms process sensitive information such as personal details, financial records, or medical data. Systems that handle such information must be designed with strong protections to prevent unauthorized access. Ethical guidelines and legal regulations often govern how data can be collected, stored, and used.

Modern technology has dramatically increased the amount of data available to computers. Every time a person sends a message, makes a purchase, or uses an online service, new data may be generated and stored. Large organizations collect and analyze this information in order to improve services, understand customer behavior, and develop new technologies. As a result, algorithms must be capable of handling enormous volumes of data efficiently.

The ability to process large datasets has led to the development of fields such as data science and artificial intelligence. These fields combine algorithms, statistics, and computing power to analyze complex information and generate insights. By examining patterns in data, algorithms can assist researchers, businesses, and governments in making informed decisions.

For students learning about computing, understanding the relationship between data and algorithms is essential. Algorithms provide the instructions that guide computation, while data provides the information that those instructions operate upon. Together, they form the foundation of modern digital systems.

As technology continues to evolve, the importance of data-driven algorithms will only increase. From healthcare diagnostics to environmental monitoring and educational technology, algorithms that analyze data are helping shape the future of many industries. By learning how data and algorithms interact, students gain a deeper understanding of the systems that power the digital world and influence everyday life.

Chapter 7 Summary

Chapter 7 explored the relationship between data and algorithms and explained how information allows computers to perform useful tasks. Algorithms provide the instructions that guide a computer's actions, but these instructions rely on data in order to produce meaningful results. Data represents information that computers can process, including numbers, text, images, sound, and measurements from sensors or devices.

Before computers can use data, the information must be represented in a digital format. Computers store and process information using binary numbers made of bits. Through different encoding systems, these bits can represent letters, numbers, images, and other types of digital content. Once information is stored in this format, algorithms can analyze and manipulate it.

The chapter discussed several important operations that algorithms perform on data. Sorting algorithms organize information into a specific order, which helps make data easier to understand and retrieve. Searching algorithms locate specific pieces of information within large datasets. These operations are essential in many computer systems, including databases, search engines, and online services.

Algorithms also use data to make decisions. Conditional instructions allow computers to examine data and choose different actions depending on the situation. For example, a program might determine whether a password is correct or whether a product is available in an online store. These decisions allow computer programs to respond to different inputs and perform useful tasks.

The chapter also introduced the role of data in artificial intelligence. AI systems learn patterns by analyzing large collections of data. Machine learning algorithms examine examples within datasets and use that information to make predictions or classifications. This ability allows AI systems to assist in fields such as healthcare, transportation, and communication.

Another important idea discussed in the chapter is the quality of data. If the information used by an algorithm is incorrect or incomplete, the results produced by the system may also be inaccurate. This principle is often summarized by the phrase "garbage in, garbage out." Ensuring that data is accurate and reliable is essential for producing trustworthy results.

Finally, the chapter addressed the importance of privacy and security when working with data. Many digital systems handle personal or sensitive information, and organizations must protect this data from misuse or unauthorized access. Responsible data practices help maintain trust and ensure that technology benefits society.

Understanding the relationship between data and algorithms helps students recognize how digital systems analyze information and make decisions. These concepts form the foundation of modern computing and play an important role in many technologies used throughout everyday life.

Reflection Questions

1. Why do algorithms require data in order to produce useful results?
2. How does binary representation allow computers to store many different types of information?
3. Why are sorting and searching important operations when working with large datasets?
4. How do algorithms use data to make decisions in computer programs?
5. Why is data quality important when designing algorithms and AI systems?

Worksheet: Data and Algorithms

Part A: Key Terms

Write a short explanation for each term.

1. Data
2. Binary representation
3. Sorting algorithm
4. Searching algorithm
5. Machine learning

Part B: Understanding Data Use

Answer the following questions.

1. Why must information be converted into digital form before computers can process it?
2. Give two examples of types of data that computers can store.
3. Why is accurate data important when algorithms are making decisions?

Part C: Data in Everyday Technology

Describe how algorithms might use data in the following situations.

1. A music streaming service recommending songs to a user.
2. A navigation system choosing the fastest driving route.
3. An online store suggesting products to customers.

Chapter 7 Quiz

1. What term describes information that a computer can process?

A. Program
B. Data
C. Device
D. Circuit

2. What number system do computers use to represent digital information?

A. Decimal
B. Binary
C. Roman
D. Fractional

3.   What type of algorithm organizes information into a specific order?

A. Sorting algorithm
B. Display algorithm
C. Input algorithm
D. Transfer algorithm

4.   What type of algorithm is used to locate specific information within a dataset?

A. Drawing algorithm
B. Searching algorithm
C. Printing algorithm
D. Encoding algorithm

5.   What phrase describes the problem that occurs when poor-quality data leads to incorrect results?

A. Double processing
B. Garbage in, garbage out
C. Parallel execution
D. Digital overflow

Quiz Answer Key

1. B — Data
2. B — Binary
3. A — Sorting algorithm
4. B — Searching algorithm
5. B — Garbage in, garbage out

Chapter 8: Efficiency in Algorithms — Solving Problems Faster

As computers solve increasingly complex problems, the efficiency of algorithms becomes critically important. Not all algorithms perform tasks in the same way or at the same speed. Two algorithms may solve the same problem but require very different amounts of time or computational resources. Because of this, computer scientists study algorithm efficiency in order to determine which solutions perform best under different conditions.

Algorithm efficiency refers to how effectively an algorithm uses resources such as time and memory while solving a problem. When an algorithm processes information quickly and uses minimal memory, it is considered efficient. If an algorithm requires excessive time or large amounts of memory to complete a task, it may be considered inefficient, especially when working with large datasets.

One reason efficiency matters is that modern computing systems often process enormous amounts of data. A small program working with only a few numbers may run quickly even if the algorithm is not very efficient. However, when a program must analyze millions or billions of pieces of information, inefficient algorithms can cause systems to slow down dramatically. In large-scale systems such as search engines, financial networks, and scientific simulations, algorithm efficiency becomes essential for maintaining reliable performance.

Computer scientists evaluate algorithm efficiency by examining how the number of operations changes as the size of the input grows. For example, imagine a program that must search for a specific name in a list of records. If the program checks each record one by one, the amount of time required increases as the list becomes larger. If the list contains only ten names, the search may be very fast. If the list contains millions of names, the same approach may become much slower.

To address this challenge, computer scientists design algorithms that reduce the number of operations required to solve a problem. For example, certain searching algorithms divide a dataset into smaller sections and eliminate large portions of the search space quickly. This strategy allows the algorithm to locate information more efficiently than examining every item individually.

Sorting algorithms provide another example of efficiency differences. Many different methods exist for organizing data into order. Some sorting algorithms compare items repeatedly, while others divide datasets into smaller groups and merge them together. Although both approaches eventually produce the correct result, one method may complete the task much faster when working with large datasets.

Another important factor in algorithm efficiency is memory usage. Some algorithms require large amounts of storage space in order to perform their calculations. Others are designed to use very little memory while still completing the task successfully. Engineers must carefully balance speed and memory usage when designing algorithms for different systems. For example, mobile devices often require algorithms that use less memory in order to conserve battery power and operate efficiently within limited hardware resources.

Computer scientists use mathematical tools to analyze how algorithms scale as input sizes grow. One widely used concept is time complexity, which describes how the running time of an algorithm increases as the amount of data increases. Instead of measuring exact seconds, time complexity focuses on how the number of steps grows relative to the size of the problem. This approach helps developers compare algorithms and choose the most appropriate solution for a particular task.

Closely related to time complexity is space complexity, which describes how much memory an algorithm requires while running. Some algorithms store additional data during execution in order to complete calculations more quickly. Others operate directly on the existing data without requiring extra storage. Understanding space complexity helps developers design systems that operate efficiently within hardware limitations.

Algorithm efficiency becomes particularly important in fields such as artificial intelligence, data science, and large-scale computing. Machine learning models may process enormous datasets containing millions of examples. Efficient algorithms allow these systems to train models faster and analyze information more effectively. Without efficient algorithms, even powerful computers could struggle to process large amounts of data.

Efficiency also affects user experience in everyday technology. When people search for information online, open applications, or stream videos, they expect results to appear quickly. Behind the scenes, algorithms are responsible for organizing data, retrieving information, and delivering results within fractions of a second. Efficient algorithms ensure that these systems respond quickly and reliably.

In addition to speed and memory usage, developers must consider the reliability and scalability of algorithms. Scalability refers to an algorithm's ability to continue functioning effectively as the amount of data grows. A scalable algorithm can handle increasing workloads without causing performance problems. This property is especially important for systems that operate on global networks, where the number of users and data points can grow rapidly.

As students learn about algorithm efficiency, they begin to understand that solving a problem correctly is only part of the challenge. The method used to reach the solution can significantly affect performance. A well-designed algorithm not only produces the correct result but does so in a way that conserves time, memory, and computing resources.

Modern technological systems rely heavily on efficient algorithms. From navigation systems that calculate optimal travel routes to recommendation engines that suggest movies or music, algorithms must analyze large datasets quickly and accurately. Engineers continually refine algorithms in order to improve performance and adapt to new technological demands.

By studying algorithm efficiency, students gain insight into how computer scientists design systems that operate at scale. They learn that careful planning and mathematical analysis play an important role in building reliable software. Understanding these principles prepares students to develop algorithms that solve problems effectively while making the best possible use of available computing resources.

In the broader context of computer science education, algorithm efficiency encourages students to think critically about problem-solving strategies. Instead of simply asking whether a solution works, they learn to ask whether it works well. This perspective helps cultivate analytical thinking and prepares future developers to design technologies capable of handling the growing complexity of the digital world.

Chapter 8 Summary

Chapter 8 examined the concept of algorithm efficiency and explained why it is important when designing computer programs. Although different algorithms may solve the same problem, they may require very different amounts of time, memory, or computing resources. Efficient algorithms complete tasks quickly while using minimal resources, making them more practical for real-world computing systems.

The chapter explained that algorithm efficiency becomes especially important when computers must process large amounts of data. While inefficient algorithms may work well with small datasets, they can slow down dramatically when the amount of data increases. Computer scientists therefore analyze how algorithms scale as the size of the input grows.

Two key measurements used to evaluate algorithm efficiency are time complexity and space complexity. Time complexity describes how the number of steps required by an algorithm increases as the dataset grows. Space complexity describes how much memory the algorithm requires while running. By studying these factors, developers can compare different algorithms and choose the most effective solution for a particular task.

The chapter also explored how algorithm efficiency affects everyday technology. Efficient algorithms allow search engines, navigation systems, and online services to process information quickly and provide results within seconds. When algorithms are inefficient, systems may become slow or unreliable.

Efficiency also influences energy usage and system scalability. Large computing systems such as data centers require significant electrical power. Efficient algorithms reduce unnecessary computations and help conserve energy. In addition, scalable algorithms allow systems to continue operating effectively as the number of users and the amount of data increase.

Finally, the chapter introduced the concept of algorithm optimization. Developers often analyze algorithms and improve them by reducing unnecessary steps or selecting better methods for solving problems. By designing efficient algorithms, engineers build software systems that perform reliably and can handle the growing demands of modern technology.

Understanding algorithm efficiency helps students recognize that solving a problem correctly is only part of the challenge. The way a solution is designed can greatly affect performance, resource usage, and system reliability.

Reflection Questions

1. Why might two algorithms that solve the same problem have different levels of efficiency?
2. Why does algorithm efficiency become more important when working with large datasets?
3. How do time complexity and space complexity help developers evaluate algorithms?
4. Why do efficient algorithms improve the performance of modern technologies such as search engines and navigation systems?
5. How can algorithm optimization improve the performance of a computer program?

Worksheet: Understanding Algorithm Efficiency

Part A: Key Terms

Write a short explanation for each term.

1. Algorithm efficiency
2. Time complexity
3. Space complexity
4. Scalability
5. Algorithm optimization

Part B: Thinking About Efficiency

Answer the following questions.

1. Why might an inefficient algorithm cause problems when processing large amounts of data?
2. Why is memory usage important when designing algorithms?
3. How can improving an algorithm reduce energy consumption in large computing systems?

Part C: Real-World Applications

Explain how algorithm efficiency is important in the following situations.

1. A search engine retrieving information from billions of webpages.
2. A navigation system calculating the fastest route for drivers.
3. A streaming service recommending movies or music to users.

Chapter 8 Quiz

1. What term describes how effectively an algorithm uses time and memory resources?

A. Algorithm efficiency
B. Data compression
C. Circuit design
D. Network speed

2. What concept describes how the running time of an algorithm increases as the input size grows?

A. Binary coding
B. Time complexity
C. Data storage
D. Memory transfer

3. What concept describes how much memory an algorithm requires while running?

A. Space complexity
B. Digital encoding
C. Data streaming
D. Network routing

4. What term describes an algorithm's ability to handle increasing amounts of data effectively?

A. Encoding
B. Scalability
C. Encryption
D. Compression

5. What process involves improving an algorithm to make it run faster or use fewer resources?

A. Translation
B. Algorithm optimization
C. Compression
D. Compilation

Quiz Answer Key

1. A — Algorithm efficiency
2. B — Time complexity

3. A — Space complexity
4. B — Scalability
5. B — Algorithm optimization

Chapter 9: Searching Algorithms — Finding Information Efficiently

One of the most common tasks performed by computers is finding specific information within large collections of data. Whether someone searches for a contact in a phone list, looks up a book in a library database, or types a question into an internet search engine, algorithms are responsible for locating the requested information. These procedures are known as searching algorithms, and they play a fundamental role in modern computing systems.

Searching algorithms are designed to examine a dataset and locate a particular value or item. A dataset may contain numbers, names, records, images, or any other form of digital information. The goal of a searching algorithm is to determine whether the desired information exists within the dataset and, if so, identify its location. Efficient searching allows computers to retrieve information quickly, even when working with very large collections of data.

One of the simplest types of searching algorithms is the linear search. In a linear search, the algorithm examines each item in a dataset one by one until it finds the desired value or reaches the end of the list. This method is straightforward and easy to implement. However, its efficiency depends heavily on the size of the dataset. If the desired item appears near the end of a long list, the algorithm may need to examine many elements before locating the correct value.

Although linear search works well for small datasets, it becomes less efficient as the amount of data increases. In large systems that store thousands or millions of records, more advanced searching techniques are often required. One such technique is the binary search algorithm.

Binary search operates differently from linear search because it requires the dataset to be organized in sorted order. Instead of examining every item individually, the algorithm repeatedly divides the dataset into smaller sections. It begins by comparing the desired value with the item located in the middle of the list. If the middle item matches the desired value, the search is complete. If the desired value is smaller, the algorithm continues searching in the first half of the dataset. If the value is larger, the search continues in the second half.

By eliminating half of the remaining dataset during each step, binary search dramatically reduces the number of comparisons required to locate an item. This approach allows the algorithm to find information much more quickly than a linear search when working with large, sorted datasets.

Searching algorithms are used in many real-world applications. Digital libraries rely on search algorithms to locate books, articles, and documents within their databases. Online stores use searching algorithms to help customers find products among thousands of available items. Social media platforms search through posts, profiles, and messages to display relevant information to users.

Search algorithms also play an important role in internet search engines. When someone enters a query into a search engine, complex algorithms analyze vast collections of webpages to locate information related to the request. These systems must search through billions of pages and deliver results within fractions of a second. Advanced indexing systems and ranking algorithms help organize and prioritize search results so that users receive relevant information quickly.

In addition to locating information, searching algorithms often work together with sorting algorithms. When datasets are sorted into a logical order, searching algorithms such as binary search become far more efficient. Many large-scale computing systems therefore organize their data carefully in order to improve search performance.

Another important concept related to searching is indexing. An index acts as a guide that helps algorithms locate information quickly without scanning the entire dataset. For example, the index at the back of a book allows readers to find specific topics without reading every page. Similarly, database systems create indexes that help computers locate records quickly within large collections of data.

Modern data systems also use specialized structures called hash tables to support extremely fast searches. A hash table uses a mathematical function to convert a key value into an index location where the associated data is stored. This approach allows computers to locate data almost instantly in many situations. Hash tables are commonly used in databases, caching systems, and many programming languages.

As computing systems continue to grow, the ability to search large datasets efficiently becomes increasingly important. Organizations store massive amounts of information related to customers, products, research, and communications. Without efficient search algorithms, locating specific information within these large datasets would be slow and difficult.

Artificial intelligence systems also rely on searching algorithms in many situations. Some AI systems search through large decision spaces in order to find optimal solutions to complex problems. For example, chess-playing programs evaluate many possible moves and use search algorithms to determine the most effective strategy. Similar techniques are used in robotics, route planning, and optimization problems.

The design of efficient searching algorithms illustrates an important principle of computer science: the structure of data often determines how efficiently it can be accessed. When information is organized carefully, algorithms can locate data quickly and reliably. Poorly organized data, on the other hand, can make searching slower and more difficult.

Understanding searching algorithms helps students appreciate how computers retrieve information from large collections of data. These algorithms enable many everyday technologies, from digital libraries and online stores to search engines and navigation systems. By studying how search algorithms work, students gain insight into how computers manage and access information efficiently in the digital age.

Searching algorithms represent another essential building block in the broader study of algorithms and data structures. As students continue learning about computer science, they will encounter more advanced techniques for organizing and retrieving information. These techniques allow modern computing systems to handle enormous datasets while maintaining fast and reliable performance.

Ultimately, searching algorithms demonstrate how carefully designed procedures can transform large collections of data into accessible and useful information. By applying logical strategies and efficient methods, computers can locate the exact information needed from vast digital environments, enabling the powerful information systems that shape modern life.

Chapter 9 Summary

Chapter 9 introduced searching algorithms and explained how computers locate specific information within large datasets. Searching is one of the most common operations performed by computer systems. Whether users are looking for a contact in a phone list, a product in an online store, or information on the internet, searching algorithms help computers find the desired data quickly and efficiently.

The chapter explained that a searching algorithm examines a dataset to determine whether a particular value or record exists and identifies its location if it does. One of the simplest search methods is linear search, where the algorithm checks each item in a list one at a time until it finds the correct value or reaches the end of the dataset. While linear search works well for small datasets, it becomes slower when the amount of data grows.

To improve efficiency, computer scientists developed more advanced search techniques such as binary search. Binary search works only with datasets that are already sorted. Instead of checking each item individually, the algorithm repeatedly divides the dataset in half. By eliminating half of the remaining data at each step, binary search can locate information much more quickly than linear search when working with large datasets.

The chapter also discussed how searching algorithms are used in many real-world applications. Online stores use search algorithms to help customers locate products, libraries use them to retrieve books and documents, and search engines rely on complex searching systems to find information across billions of webpages. These technologies depend on efficient algorithms in order to provide results quickly.

Another important concept introduced in the chapter is indexing. An index allows computers to locate information quickly without scanning an entire dataset. Similar to the index in a book, database indexes help systems find specific records faster. The chapter also briefly introduced hash tables, which use mathematical functions to determine where data is stored so that it can be retrieved rapidly.

Understanding searching algorithms helps students see how computers manage and retrieve information from large collections of data. Efficient search techniques make modern digital systems possible by allowing users to access information quickly even when datasets contain millions or billions of records.

Reflection Questions

1. Why are searching algorithms important in modern computing systems?
2. How does linear search locate information within a dataset?
3. Why is binary search more efficient than linear search for large sorted datasets?
4. How do search engines and online services rely on searching algorithms?
5. Why do indexing systems help computers retrieve information more quickly?

Worksheet: Searching Algorithms

Part A: Key Terms

Write a short explanation for each term.

1. Searching algorithm
2. Linear search
3. Binary search
4. Index
5. Hash table

Part B: Understanding Search Methods

Answer the following questions.

1. What happens during a linear search when the desired item is near the end of a long list?
2. Why must data be sorted before using binary search?
3. How does binary search reduce the number of comparisons needed to find a value?

Part C: Real-World Searching

Explain how searching algorithms help in the following situations.

1. Finding a contact in a smartphone address book.
2. Searching for a product in an online store.
3. Retrieving information from a digital library.

Chapter 9 Quiz

1. What type of algorithm is used to locate specific information within a dataset?

A. Sorting algorithm
B. Searching algorithm
C. Display algorithm
D. Compression algorithm

2. What searching method examines each item in a dataset one at a time?

A. Binary search
B. Linear search
C. Parallel search
D. Index search

3. What requirement must be met before binary search can be used?

A. The dataset must be encrypted
B. The dataset must be sorted
C. The dataset must be compressed
D. The dataset must be duplicated

4. What tool helps computers find information quickly in large databases without scanning every record?

A. Display system
B. Index
C. Circuit
D. Keyboard

5. What data structure uses a mathematical function to determine where information is stored?

A. Stack
B. Hash table
C. Queue
D. Array

Quiz Answer Key

1. B — Searching algorithm

2. B — Linear search
3. B — The dataset must be sorted
4. B — Index
5. B — Hash table

Chapter 10: Sorting Algorithms — Organizing Information for Faster Access

As computers process large collections of data, organizing that information becomes essential for efficiency and usability. When data is arranged in a logical order, it becomes easier for algorithms to search, analyze, and interpret the information. Sorting algorithms are the procedures used by computers to arrange data in a specific sequence, such as numerical order, alphabetical order, or chronological order.

Sorting is one of the most fundamental operations in computer science. Many computer programs rely on sorted data to function effectively. For example, digital contact lists are typically arranged alphabetically so that users can quickly locate a name. Financial records may be sorted by date or transaction amount, while scientific data may be organized according to measurements or experimental results. Sorting allows large datasets to be structured in ways that make them easier to manage and interpret.

A sorting algorithm works by comparing elements in a dataset and rearranging them until they appear in the desired order. These elements may represent numbers, words, or records containing multiple pieces of information. Although the goal of every sorting algorithm is the same, the methods used to achieve this goal can differ significantly.

One of the simplest sorting methods is the bubble sort algorithm. In bubble sort, the algorithm repeatedly compares adjacent elements in a list and swaps them if they are in the wrong order. With each pass through the dataset, larger values gradually move toward the end of the list, similar to bubbles rising to the surface of water. While bubble sort is easy to understand and implement, it becomes inefficient when working with large datasets because it requires many repeated comparisons.

Another commonly studied sorting method is selection sort. In this approach, the algorithm repeatedly searches for the smallest value in the unsorted portion of the dataset and moves it to its correct position in the sorted portion of the list. This process continues until all elements have been arranged in order. Selection sort improves organization step by step, gradually expanding the sorted portion of the dataset.

Insertion sort uses a different strategy. Instead of searching for the smallest element, the algorithm builds a sorted list one element at a time. Each new element is compared with items already in the sorted portion and inserted into the correct position. This method is similar to how people often sort playing cards in their hands by placing each card into its appropriate position.

Although these simple algorithms are useful for learning the principles of sorting, computer scientists have developed more advanced algorithms that perform much more efficiently when handling large datasets. One such algorithm is merge sort. Merge sort divides a dataset into smaller sections, sorts each section independently, and then merges the sections back together in the correct order. By breaking the problem into smaller parts, merge sort can handle large datasets more efficiently than simpler sorting methods.

Another highly efficient sorting algorithm is quicksort. Quicksort works by selecting a value known as a pivot and dividing the dataset into two groups: elements smaller than the pivot and elements larger than the pivot. Each group is then sorted separately using the same method. This divide-and-conquer strategy allows quicksort to sort large datasets quickly and efficiently.

Sorting algorithms are used in many real-world applications. Online stores sort products based on price, popularity, or customer ratings. Email systems sort messages by date or sender. Music streaming platforms organize playlists by artist or album. In each case, sorting algorithms help structure large collections of data so that users can find information quickly and easily.

Sorting also improves the performance of other algorithms. Many searching techniques, such as binary search, rely on sorted data in order to function efficiently. When datasets are organized properly, searching algorithms can locate information much faster. As a result, sorting often serves as a preparation step before other types of data processing occur.

In large computing systems, sorting algorithms are used to organize enormous datasets. Data centers may process information related to financial transactions, scientific research, healthcare records, and global communication networks. Efficient sorting algorithms allow these systems to handle large volumes of information while maintaining reliable performance.

Algorithm designers must consider several factors when selecting a sorting method. These factors include the size of the dataset, the amount of available memory, and the speed requirements of the system. In some situations, simple sorting algorithms may be sufficient. In others, advanced algorithms are necessary to maintain efficiency when processing millions or billions of data items.

Sorting algorithms also demonstrate an important concept in computer science known as algorithm trade-offs. Some algorithms may require less memory but take longer to run, while others may complete tasks quickly but use more memory. Engineers must carefully evaluate these trade-offs when designing systems that must operate efficiently under different conditions.

Understanding sorting algorithms helps students appreciate how computers organize information behind the scenes. Many everyday technologies rely on sorting processes to deliver information in a structured and accessible format. By learning how these algorithms work, students gain insight into how computers manage large datasets and support the digital systems used throughout modern society.

Sorting algorithms represent another essential building block in the broader study of algorithms and data structures. As students continue learning about computing, they will encounter additional techniques for organizing and managing information. These concepts form the foundation for many advanced technologies, including data analytics, artificial intelligence, and large-scale information systems.

Ultimately, sorting algorithms demonstrate how carefully designed procedures allow computers to transform disorganized data into structured information. By arranging data in meaningful ways, these algorithms make it possible for digital systems to process information efficiently and deliver useful results to users around the world.

Chapter 10 Summary

Chapter 10 introduced sorting algorithms and explained how computers organize data so it can be accessed and analyzed more efficiently. Sorting is a fundamental process in computing because many systems depend on structured information in order to function effectively. When data is arranged in a logical order, such as alphabetical or numerical order, it becomes easier for algorithms to search, compare, and process information.

The chapter explained that sorting algorithms work by comparing elements within a dataset and rearranging them until the desired order is achieved. These elements may represent numbers, words, or records containing multiple pieces of information. Although many sorting algorithms accomplish the same goal, they may differ greatly in how efficiently they perform the task.

Several common sorting methods were introduced. Bubble sort repeatedly compares adjacent elements and swaps them if they are in the wrong order. Selection sort repeatedly identifies the smallest remaining element and moves it to its correct position. Insertion sort builds a sorted list gradually by inserting each element into its appropriate place within the ordered portion of the dataset.

The chapter also described more advanced sorting algorithms designed for large datasets. Merge sort divides the dataset into smaller parts, sorts each part, and then combines them into a final ordered list. Quicksort uses a pivot value to divide the dataset into smaller groups and then sorts those groups recursively. These advanced algorithms are widely used because they can organize large datasets much more efficiently than simpler methods.

Sorting algorithms are used in many everyday technologies. Email systems organize messages by date, online stores sort products by price or popularity, and music platforms arrange playlists by artist or album. Sorting also improves the efficiency of searching algorithms, since many search techniques require data to be arranged in order before they can operate effectively.

By studying sorting algorithms, students learn how computers transform unorganized data into structured information. These techniques allow digital systems to manage large collections of data and provide users with quick access to the information they need.

Reflection Questions

1. Why is sorting important when working with large datasets?
2. How do sorting algorithms help improve the efficiency of searching algorithms?
3. Why might different sorting algorithms perform differently when working with large amounts of data?
4. How do sorting algorithms help organize information in everyday technologies such as email systems or online stores?
5. Why do computer scientists continue to develop new sorting algorithms for modern computing systems?

Worksheet: Sorting Algorithms

Part A: Key Terms

Write a short explanation for each term.

1. Sorting algorithm
2. Bubble sort
3. Selection sort
4. Merge sort
5. Quicksort

Part B: Understanding Sorting

Answer the following questions.

1. What is the main purpose of a sorting algorithm?
2. Why might bubble sort become inefficient when working with large datasets?
3. How does merge sort improve efficiency by dividing data into smaller parts?

Part C: Everyday Examples

Describe how sorting algorithms are used in the following situations.

1. Organizing contacts in a smartphone alphabetically.
2. Displaying products in an online store from lowest price to highest price.
3. Sorting email messages by the date they were received.

Chapter 10 Quiz

1. What is the main purpose of a sorting algorithm?

A. To store data
B. To arrange data in a specific order
C. To delete information
D. To display images

2. Which sorting method repeatedly swaps adjacent elements that are out of order?

A. Bubble sort
B. Binary sort
C. Network sort
D. Cluster sort

3. Which sorting algorithm builds a sorted list one element at a time by inserting elements into their correct positions?

A. Selection sort
B. Insertion sort
C. Merge sort
D. Quick sort

4. Which advanced sorting algorithm divides data into smaller sections and then merges them together?

A. Bubble sort
B. Merge sort
C. Linear sort
D. Sequential sort

5. What value does quicksort use to divide the dataset into smaller groups?

A. Anchor
B. Pivot
C. Segment
D. Factor

Quiz Answer Key

1. B — To arrange data in a specific order
2. A — Bubble sort
3. B — Insertion sort
4. B — Merge sort
5. B — Pivot

Chapter 11: Decision-Making in Algorithms — How Computers Choose What to Do

In many situations, solving a problem requires more than simply following a fixed sequence of steps. Often a system must evaluate information and decide between multiple possible actions. Decision-making is therefore an essential feature of algorithms. It allows computer programs to respond differently depending on the conditions they encounter.

Decision-making in algorithms is based on logical evaluation. A computer examines a condition and determines whether that condition is true or false. Depending on the outcome, the algorithm follows one path or another. This process allows computer systems to adapt their behavior to different inputs and situations.

A simple example of decision-making can be seen in a program that checks whether a user has entered the correct password. When a person attempts to log in, the system compares the entered password with the stored password. If the two values match, the program allows access. If they do not match, the system denies access and may request the password again. This decision is made by evaluating a condition and choosing the appropriate response.

Conditional statements are the instructions that allow algorithms to make decisions. These statements instruct the computer to perform an action only if a particular condition is satisfied. The most common form of conditional logic is the "if" statement. An if statement checks whether a condition is true and executes a set of instructions when that condition is met.

In some cases, an algorithm must choose between two different actions. This situation is often handled using an "if–else" structure. The algorithm first evaluates the condition. If the condition is true, one action occurs. If the condition is false, an alternative action takes place. This structure allows programs to respond to different outcomes in a clear and organized way.

More complex decision-making may involve multiple conditions. In these situations, algorithms may use a structure that evaluates several possible cases. The system checks each condition in sequence and performs the action associated with the first condition that evaluates as true. This approach allows algorithms to handle a wide range of scenarios.

Decision-making is used in many everyday technologies. Navigation systems use decision logic to determine whether a driver should take a different route based on traffic conditions. Online shopping platforms decide whether a product is available in stock before completing a purchase. Email filters examine incoming messages and decide whether they should be placed in an inbox or a spam folder.

Artificial intelligence systems also rely heavily on decision-making algorithms. Machine learning models analyze large amounts of data and make predictions or classifications based on patterns they detect. For example, an AI system designed to recognize images may decide whether a picture contains a specific object. Although these systems may appear highly intelligent, they ultimately rely on structured decision processes based on mathematical models.

Decision-making algorithms are also used in automated systems that must respond quickly to changing conditions. For example, safety systems in modern vehicles monitor sensor data and make decisions about braking or stability control. Medical monitoring devices analyze patient data and alert healthcare professionals when abnormal conditions are detected. In these situations, reliable decision-making algorithms can play an important role in protecting safety and well-being.

When designing algorithms that involve decisions, programmers must carefully define the conditions that determine each outcome. Clear logical rules help ensure that the system behaves predictably and consistently. Poorly defined conditions may cause a program to behave incorrectly or produce unexpected results.

Another important aspect of decision-making in algorithms is testing. Developers must examine many possible scenarios to ensure that the algorithm responds correctly in each case. Testing helps identify errors in logic and ensures that programs behave reliably under different conditions.

Decision-making also contributes to the adaptability of computer systems. Programs that incorporate conditional logic can handle a wide variety of inputs without requiring separate programs for each situation. This flexibility allows a single algorithm to support many different tasks and environments.

In addition to logical correctness, decision-making algorithms must often consider fairness and ethical responsibility. Systems that make decisions about loans, employment, or healthcare must be designed carefully to avoid bias and ensure fair outcomes. Responsible design practices help ensure that decision-making technologies serve society in a positive and equitable manner.

Understanding decision-making in algorithms helps students recognize how computers respond to changing conditions and solve problems that require judgment. Although computers do not possess human reasoning or intuition, conditional logic allows them to evaluate information and select appropriate actions.

By studying decision-making algorithms, students gain insight into how computer programs adapt to different situations. This knowledge helps explain how modern technologies—from navigation systems to artificial intelligence applications—use structured logical rules to process information and make choices.

Decision-making represents another important building block in algorithm design. Together with sequencing, repetition, searching, and sorting, decision-making enables algorithms to handle complex tasks and respond intelligently to different inputs. These principles form the foundation of many computing systems that shape the digital world.

Chapter 11 Summary

Chapter 11 explored how algorithms make decisions when solving problems. Many computer programs cannot simply follow a fixed sequence of instructions. Instead, they must evaluate conditions and choose between different actions depending on the situation. This ability to evaluate conditions and select outcomes is known as decision-making in algorithms.

The chapter explained that decision-making is based on logical evaluation. Computers examine conditions that can be either true or false. Based on the result of that evaluation, the algorithm follows a particular path of instructions. Conditional statements allow programs to respond differently depending on the input they receive.

One of the most common tools used for decision-making is the **if statement**, which allows a program to perform an action only when a certain condition is true. In situations where two different outcomes are possible, programmers often use an **if–else structure**. This structure allows the algorithm to perform one action if a condition is true and a different action if the condition is false.

More complex systems may evaluate multiple conditions before determining which action to perform. This allows algorithms to handle a wide range of possible scenarios. Decision-making structures help computer programs adapt to different inputs, making them more flexible and capable of solving complex problems.

The chapter also discussed real-world applications of algorithmic decision-making. Navigation systems analyze traffic conditions to determine the best route. Online stores check whether products are in stock before completing a purchase. Email services evaluate messages and decide whether they belong in the inbox or spam folder.

Artificial intelligence systems also rely heavily on decision-making processes. Machine learning models analyze data and classify information based on patterns they identify. Although these systems can perform complex tasks, their decisions are ultimately based on structured logical rules and mathematical models.

Finally, the chapter emphasized the importance of careful design and testing in decision-making algorithms. Programmers must ensure that conditions are clearly defined and that programs respond correctly under different circumstances. Responsible design practices also help ensure fairness and prevent unintended bias in systems that make important decisions.

Understanding decision-making in algorithms helps students recognize how computers evaluate information and select appropriate actions. These logical processes allow modern technologies to adapt to changing conditions and support many everyday digital systems.

Reflection Questions

1. Why is decision-making important in computer algorithms?
2. How do conditional statements allow programs to respond to different situations?
3. What is the difference between an **if statement** and an **if–else structure**?
4. How do everyday technologies use decision-making algorithms?

5. Why is it important to test algorithms that involve decision-making?

Worksheet: Decision-Making in Algorithms

Part A: Key Terms

Write a short explanation for each term.

1. Conditional statement
2. If statement
3. If–else structure
4. Logical condition
5. Decision-making algorithm

Part B: Understanding Conditions

Answer the following questions.

1. What two outcomes can a logical condition produce?
2. Why do algorithms need decision-making capabilities?
3. Give an example of a situation where a computer program must choose between two actions.

Part C: Algorithm Decisions in Daily Life

Explain how decision-making algorithms might be used in the following situations.

1. A smartphone unlocking when the correct passcode is entered.
2. A streaming service recommending movies to viewers.
3. A weather application issuing severe weather alerts.

Chapter 11 Quiz

1. What allows an algorithm to choose between different actions?

A. Storage
B. Decision-making

C. Compression
D. Encryption

2. What type of statement checks whether a condition is true before performing an action?

A. Loop statement
B. If statement
C. Sorting statement
D. Display statement

3. What structure allows an algorithm to perform one action if a condition is true and another action if it is false?

A. If–else structure
B. Binary structure
C. Sorting structure
D. Storage structure

4. What type of value is typically evaluated in algorithm conditions?

A. Random values
B. True or false values
C. Infinite values
D. Circular values

5. Which technology commonly uses decision-making algorithms to determine the best route?

A. Navigation system
B. Printer
C. Calculator
D. Speaker

Quiz Answer Key

1. B — Decision-making
2. B — If statement
3. A — If–else structure
4. B — True or false values
5. A — Navigation system

Chapter 12: Algorithms and Artificial Intelligence — Learning from Data

As computing technology continues to advance, algorithms have become the foundation of many intelligent systems. Artificial intelligence, often called AI, relies heavily on algorithms that analyze data, recognize patterns, and make predictions. While traditional algorithms follow clearly defined instructions, many AI algorithms are designed to learn from data and improve their performance over time.

Artificial intelligence does not represent a single technology but rather a collection of methods that allow computers to perform tasks that normally require human intelligence. These tasks may include recognizing speech, identifying objects in images, translating languages, or recommending products to users. At the center of these capabilities are algorithms that analyze large amounts of information in order to detect patterns and relationships.

Traditional algorithms typically operate with explicit instructions written by programmers. For example, a program that calculates the average of several numbers follows a specific sequence of steps that always produce the same result for the same input. In contrast, many AI systems rely on algorithms that learn patterns from data rather than following a rigid set of predefined rules.

Machine learning is one of the most important branches of artificial intelligence. In machine learning systems, algorithms are trained using large datasets that contain examples of the task the system is expected to perform. By analyzing these examples, the algorithm gradually learns how to make predictions or classifications based on new data.

For instance, an image recognition system may be trained using thousands or millions of labeled images. Each image might include information indicating what object appears in the picture. Over time, the algorithm learns to recognize patterns in the images that correspond to different objects. When the system encounters a new image, it can analyze the visual features and determine what object is most likely present.

Another example of machine learning can be found in recommendation systems used by online platforms. Streaming services analyze user preferences and viewing history in order to recommend movies or music that users may enjoy. The algorithms examine patterns across large numbers of users and identify similarities in behavior. Based on these patterns, the system generates personalized recommendations.

Artificial intelligence algorithms often rely on structures known as neural networks. Neural networks are computational models inspired by the structure of the human brain. They consist of interconnected units that process information and pass signals to other units within the network. By adjusting the strength of these connections during training, the system gradually improves its ability to perform a task.

Deep learning is a specialized form of machine learning that uses large neural networks with many layers. These networks are capable of learning highly complex patterns within data. Deep learning algorithms have enabled major advances in areas such as speech recognition, natural language processing, and computer vision.

Although AI systems may appear intelligent, it is important to understand that they do not think or understand information in the same way humans do. Instead, they rely on mathematical algorithms that analyze patterns in data and produce outputs based on those patterns. The effectiveness of these systems depends heavily on the quality and quantity of the data used during training.

Data plays a critical role in artificial intelligence. Machine learning algorithms require large datasets in order to identify patterns and make accurate predictions. If the data used for training is incomplete, biased, or inaccurate, the resulting system may produce unreliable or unfair results. For this reason, responsible data collection and careful evaluation of datasets are essential components of AI development.

Another important consideration in AI systems is model training. During the training process, algorithms adjust internal parameters in order to minimize errors in their predictions. This process often involves evaluating the system's performance on many examples and gradually improving accuracy through repeated adjustments. Once training is complete, the model can be used to analyze new data and generate predictions.

Artificial intelligence is used in many areas of modern society. In healthcare, AI algorithms assist doctors in analyzing medical images and identifying possible diseases. In transportation, AI systems help optimize traffic patterns and support autonomous vehicles. In finance, algorithms analyze transactions to detect fraud and manage financial risks.

AI technologies are also widely used in education. Intelligent tutoring systems can analyze student performance and provide personalized learning experiences. Language translation systems allow people from different parts of the world to communicate more easily. Virtual assistants help users perform tasks such as scheduling appointments or answering questions.

Despite these advances, artificial intelligence also raises important ethical and social questions. Developers must consider issues such as fairness, privacy, transparency, and accountability when designing AI systems. Responsible development practices help ensure that these technologies benefit society while minimizing potential risks.

Understanding how algorithms power artificial intelligence helps students see the connection between foundational computer science concepts and modern technological systems. The algorithms studied in earlier chapters—such as searching, sorting, and decision-making—form the building blocks that support more advanced AI systems.

As technology continues to evolve, algorithms that learn from data will play an increasingly important role in shaping the future. By studying these systems, students gain insight into how computers analyze information, recognize patterns, and assist humans in solving complex problems.

Artificial intelligence represents a powerful extension of algorithmic thinking. While traditional algorithms follow explicit instructions, AI systems use algorithms that adapt and improve through experience. Together, these approaches demonstrate how carefully designed computational methods allow computers to process information and support innovation across many areas of modern life.

Chapter 12 Summary

Chapter 12 introduced the relationship between algorithms and artificial intelligence. Artificial intelligence systems rely on algorithms to analyze data, detect patterns, and generate predictions. While traditional algorithms follow clear instructions written by programmers, many AI algorithms learn from data and improve their performance over time.

The chapter explained that machine learning is a major branch of artificial intelligence. In machine learning systems, algorithms are trained using large datasets that contain examples of the task the system must perform. By studying these examples, the algorithm learns patterns that help it make predictions when new data is presented.

Neural networks are an important structure used in many AI systems. Inspired by the structure of the human brain, neural networks consist of connected processing units that pass information between layers. Through a training process, the system adjusts internal parameters to improve accuracy. Deep learning systems extend this concept by using many layers in the network, allowing them to recognize highly complex patterns.

The chapter also discussed practical applications of AI algorithms. AI systems assist in image recognition, speech processing, language translation, recommendation systems, healthcare diagnostics, and many other fields. These systems analyze large datasets in order to provide useful insights and automate tasks.

Another key concept introduced in the chapter is the importance of data quality. AI systems depend heavily on the data used during training. If the training data is incomplete, inaccurate, or biased, the algorithm may produce incorrect or unfair results. Responsible data practices and careful system design are therefore essential in AI development.

The chapter also emphasized that although AI systems can perform complex tasks, they do not possess human understanding or consciousness. Their behavior is the result of mathematical algorithms that analyze patterns in data. Understanding this distinction helps students better appreciate the capabilities and limitations of artificial intelligence technologies.

Reflection Questions

1. How do artificial intelligence algorithms differ from traditional algorithms?
2. Why is machine learning an important part of modern AI systems?
3. How do neural networks help computers recognize patterns in data?

4. Why is the quality of training data important when developing AI systems?
5. What are some examples of how AI algorithms are used in everyday technology?

Worksheet: Algorithms and Artificial Intelligence

Part A: Key Terms

Write a short explanation for each term.

1. Artificial Intelligence (AI)
2. Machine Learning
3. Neural Network
4. Deep Learning
5. Training Data

Part B: Understanding AI Systems

Answer the following questions.

1. How do machine learning algorithms improve their performance over time?
2. Why do AI systems require large datasets during training?
3. What might happen if an AI system is trained using inaccurate or biased data?

Part C: AI in the Real World

Explain how AI algorithms may be used in the following situations.

1. A smartphone recognizing a user's face to unlock the device.
2. A streaming platform recommending movies or music to users.
3. A healthcare system analyzing medical images to detect diseases.

Chapter 12 Quiz

1. What field of technology uses algorithms that learn patterns from data?

A. Artificial Intelligence
B. Mechanical Engineering

C. Electrical Wiring
D. Graphic Design

2. What branch of AI involves training algorithms using large datasets?

A. Data transfer
B. Machine learning
C. Hardware design
D. Network routing

3. What type of computational model is inspired by the structure of the human brain?

A. Binary circuit
B. Neural network
C. Storage device
D. Input system

4. What term describes the process of improving an AI model by adjusting its internal parameters using data?

A. Encryption
B. Training
C. Compression
D. Formatting

5. Why is high-quality data important for AI systems?

A. It improves screen brightness
B. It ensures reliable and fair results
C. It reduces electricity costs
D. It increases file size

Quiz Answer Key

1. A — Artificial Intelligence
2. B — Machine learning
3. B — Neural network
4. B — Training
5. B — It ensures reliable and fair results

Chapter 13: Ethics and Responsibility in Algorithm Design

As algorithms become increasingly integrated into everyday life, their influence on society continues to grow. Algorithms help determine which information appears in search results, which products are recommended to consumers, and even how certain decisions are made in areas such as finance, healthcare, and transportation. Because algorithms affect many aspects of modern life, it is important for developers, organizations, and users to consider the ethical responsibilities associated with designing and using these systems.

Ethics refers to principles that guide decisions about what is fair, responsible, and appropriate. In the context of computing, ethical considerations help ensure that algorithms serve society in a positive and responsible way. When algorithms are designed without careful attention to ethical principles, they may produce outcomes that are unfair, misleading, or harmful.

One important ethical concern in algorithm design is bias. Bias occurs when an algorithm produces results that systematically favor or disadvantage certain individuals or groups. Bias can appear in algorithms for many reasons, but one common source is the data used to train or develop the system. If the data used by an algorithm reflects existing inequalities or lacks diversity, the algorithm may learn patterns that unintentionally reinforce those inequalities.

For example, consider an algorithm designed to evaluate job applications. If the data used to train the algorithm primarily reflects the hiring patterns of a specific group or organization, the algorithm may favor certain characteristics while overlooking others. This can lead to unfair outcomes and reduce opportunities for qualified candidates. Addressing bias requires careful data selection, testing, and evaluation throughout the development process.

Transparency is another important ethical principle in algorithm design. Transparency refers to the ability to understand how an algorithm makes decisions. Some algorithms, particularly those used in complex artificial intelligence systems, may be difficult to interpret. When decisions affect people's lives, such as loan approvals or medical diagnoses, it is important for developers and organizations to provide clear explanations of how those decisions are made.

Accountability is closely related to transparency. When algorithms influence important outcomes, there must be clear responsibility for their behavior. Developers, organizations, and regulators all play roles in ensuring that algorithms operate fairly and responsibly. Establishing accountability helps ensure that systems can be evaluated, corrected, and improved when problems arise.

Privacy is another critical concern when designing algorithms that process personal data. Many digital systems collect and analyze large amounts of information about users. This data may include personal details, online activity, location information, or communication records. Developers must design algorithms that protect sensitive data and respect individuals' privacy rights.

Security is also an essential consideration. Algorithms often operate within systems that manage financial transactions, healthcare records, and other sensitive information. Weak security measures can expose these systems to unauthorized access or malicious attacks. Designing algorithms with strong security protections helps ensure that digital systems remain safe and trustworthy.

Ethical algorithm design also involves considering the broader impact of technology on society. For example, automation powered by algorithms may increase efficiency and productivity in many industries. However, it may also affect employment patterns as certain tasks become automated. Responsible technology development involves considering both the benefits and the potential consequences of these changes.

Developers must also consider fairness when designing algorithmic systems. Fairness involves ensuring that algorithms treat individuals and groups equitably. This may require testing algorithms across diverse datasets and evaluating whether outcomes remain consistent across different populations. Fairness is particularly important in areas such as healthcare, criminal justice, and financial services, where algorithmic decisions can have significant real-world consequences.

Another important concept in ethical algorithm design is explainability. Explainable systems allow users and experts to understand how an algorithm arrives at a particular decision. When algorithms operate as "black boxes" with little explanation, it can be difficult to evaluate their behavior or correct errors. Improving explainability helps build trust between technology developers and the communities that rely on their systems.

Governments, researchers, and organizations around the world are increasingly developing guidelines and policies to promote responsible AI and algorithm development. These frameworks encourage transparency, fairness, accountability, and privacy protection. By following ethical guidelines, developers can help ensure that algorithms are used in ways that benefit society while minimizing risks.

Education also plays a critical role in responsible technology development. Students learning about algorithms and artificial intelligence should understand not only the technical aspects of these systems but also their social and ethical implications. Developing ethical awareness helps future engineers and scientists create technologies that serve the public interest.

The growing influence of algorithms means that ethical decision-making will remain an important part of technology development. As algorithms continue to shape communication, commerce, education, and healthcare, responsible design practices will help ensure that these systems remain trustworthy and beneficial.

Understanding ethics in algorithm design allows students to recognize that technology is not neutral. The choices made by developers influence how systems behave and how they affect society. By considering fairness, transparency, accountability, and privacy, algorithm designers can help build technologies that promote trust, safety, and responsible innovation.

Ultimately, ethical algorithm design reflects the shared responsibility of those who create and use technology. Algorithms are powerful tools that can improve many aspects of human life, but their impact depends on how thoughtfully they are designed and applied. By combining technical knowledge with ethical awareness, future developers can contribute to building systems that support both innovation and social responsibility.

Chapter 13 Summary

Chapter 13 explored the ethical responsibilities involved in designing and using algorithms. As algorithms become more integrated into everyday technology, their influence on society continues to expand. Algorithms help determine search results, recommend products, support healthcare decisions, and assist in financial systems. Because these systems can affect people's lives, it is important to design them responsibly and ethically.

One of the key ethical concerns discussed in the chapter is **bias**. Bias occurs when an algorithm produces unfair outcomes that favor or disadvantage certain groups. Bias can often result from the data used to train or develop an algorithm. If the data contains historical inequalities or lacks diversity, the algorithm may learn patterns that unintentionally reinforce those inequalities. Developers must therefore carefully evaluate the data used in algorithm design.

The chapter also emphasized the importance of **transparency**. Transparency allows users and experts to understand how algorithms make decisions. When algorithms influence important outcomes—such as loan approvals or medical recommendations—it is essential that their decision-making processes can be explained and evaluated.

Closely related to transparency is **accountability**. When algorithms are used in critical systems, there must be clear responsibility for how those systems operate. Developers, organizations, and regulators share the responsibility of ensuring that algorithmic systems behave fairly and reliably.

Another major ethical consideration is **privacy**. Many algorithms process personal data, including user preferences, location information, and communication records. Responsible system design requires protecting this data and respecting individuals' rights to privacy. Strong security practices are also necessary to prevent unauthorized access to sensitive information.

The chapter also discussed **fairness and explainability** in algorithm design. Fairness ensures that algorithms treat individuals and groups equitably, while explainability allows people to understand how decisions are made. These principles help build trust in technological systems.

Finally, the chapter highlighted the role of education in preparing future developers to consider ethical issues in technology. Understanding ethical responsibilities helps students recognize that algorithms are powerful tools whose impact depends on how thoughtfully they are designed and used.

Reflection Questions

1. Why is it important to consider ethics when designing algorithms?
2. How can bias appear in algorithmic systems?
3. Why is transparency important when algorithms influence important decisions?
4. How do privacy and security affect the design of modern algorithms?
5. Why should students studying computer science learn about ethical responsibility?

Worksheet: Ethics in Algorithm Design

Part A: Key Terms

Write a short explanation for each term.

1. Algorithmic bias
2. Transparency
3. Accountability
4. Privacy
5. Explainability

Part B: Ethical Thinking

Answer the following questions.

1. Why might an algorithm produce unfair results if it is trained with incomplete or biased data?
2. Why should organizations explain how their algorithms make decisions?
3. How can developers help ensure fairness in algorithm design?

Part C: Real-World Ethical Scenarios

Explain the ethical considerations in the following situations.

1. A hiring system that uses algorithms to evaluate job applicants.
2. A healthcare system that uses AI to help diagnose diseases.
3. A social media platform that uses algorithms to recommend content to users.

Chapter 13 Quiz

1. What term describes unfair outcomes that occur when an algorithm favors or disadvantages certain groups?

A. Compression
B. Bias
C. Encryption
D. Translation

2. What principle allows people to understand how an algorithm makes decisions?

A. Transparency
B. Compression
C. Storage
D. Routing

3. What concept ensures that organizations are responsible for how their algorithms behave?

A. Compression
B. Encryption
C. Accountability
D. Formatting

4. What ethical concern involves protecting personal information processed by algorithms?

A. Privacy
B. Rendering
C. Calibration
D. Synchronization

5. What concept refers to the ability to explain how an algorithm arrives at a decision?

A. Execution
B. Explainability
C. Formatting
D. Compilation

Quiz Answer Key

1. B — Bias
2. A — Transparency
3. C — Accountability
4. A — Privacy
5. B — Explainability

Chapter 14: Algorithms in the Real World — Applications Across Industries

Algorithms are not just theoretical concepts studied in computer science classrooms. They are practical tools used in countless technologies that shape modern life. From smartphones and navigation systems to medical diagnostics and financial services, algorithms help process information, solve problems, and support decision-making in a wide variety of industries.

One of the most visible applications of algorithms appears in search engines. When a user enters a query into an internet search engine, the system must analyze billions of webpages to determine which results are most relevant. This process involves multiple algorithms that index webpages, analyze keywords, evaluate links between pages, and rank results based on relevance and credibility. These algorithms work together to deliver useful information within fractions of a second.

Another area where algorithms play a major role is navigation and transportation systems. Modern navigation applications analyze real-time traffic data, road conditions, and route distances in order to recommend the fastest path to a destination. These systems rely on algorithms that evaluate multiple route options and calculate the most efficient path based on current conditions.

Algorithms are also essential in financial systems. Banks and financial institutions use algorithms to process transactions, detect fraud, and manage investment portfolios. Fraud detection systems analyze patterns of financial activity to identify unusual transactions that may indicate unauthorized activity. Investment algorithms analyze market data to help guide trading decisions and manage financial risk.

Healthcare is another field where algorithms are making significant contributions. Medical imaging systems use algorithms to analyze X-rays, MRI scans, and other diagnostic images. These algorithms can assist doctors by highlighting potential abnormalities that require further examination. In addition, predictive algorithms can analyze patient data to help identify health risks and recommend preventive care strategies.

In the field of education, algorithms help personalize learning experiences for students. Educational platforms analyze student performance data in order to adjust lessons, recommend additional practice exercises, and provide feedback tailored to each learner's needs. These systems help educators identify areas where students may need additional support.

Retail and e-commerce industries also depend heavily on algorithms. Online stores analyze customer behavior, purchase history, and browsing patterns to recommend products that customers may find interesting. Pricing algorithms may adjust product prices based on demand, availability, and market conditions. These systems help businesses respond quickly to changing consumer preferences.

Social media platforms use algorithms to determine which content appears in a user's feed. These systems analyze user interactions, interests, and engagement patterns in order to prioritize posts that are likely to be relevant or interesting. While these algorithms can help users discover new content, they also raise important questions about how information is filtered and presented.

Algorithms also support many modern communication technologies. Email systems use algorithms to filter spam messages and organize incoming communications. Video streaming platforms use algorithms to adjust video quality based on internet connection speed. Language translation systems analyze text in different languages and generate translations that allow people to communicate across cultural boundaries.

In the field of logistics and supply chain management, algorithms help coordinate the movement of goods across complex transportation networks. Shipping companies use algorithms to optimize delivery routes, schedule shipments, and track inventory across warehouses and distribution centers. Efficient algorithms allow these systems to deliver products quickly and reduce operational costs.

Scientific research also relies heavily on algorithms. Researchers use algorithms to analyze large datasets collected from experiments, simulations, and observations. In fields such as climate science, astronomy, and genetics, algorithms help scientists detect patterns and generate insights from enormous amounts of data.

Another rapidly growing area of algorithm application is robotics and automation. Robots rely on algorithms to process sensor information, navigate environments, and perform tasks with precision. Autonomous vehicles, for example, use algorithms to interpret data from cameras, radar, and other sensors in order to make driving decisions.

Artificial intelligence systems integrate many different types of algorithms to perform complex tasks. Machine learning algorithms analyze data to recognize patterns, natural language processing algorithms interpret human language, and computer vision algorithms analyze images and videos. Together, these technologies enable systems that can assist humans in many areas of work and daily life.

Despite their many benefits, real-world applications of algorithms also require careful oversight. Because algorithms influence so many aspects of society, developers must ensure that systems are reliable, transparent, and ethically designed. Responsible development practices help ensure that algorithmic systems serve the public interest.

Understanding how algorithms operate in real-world environments helps students see the practical impact of computer science. Algorithms are not simply abstract procedures; they are tools that support many of the technologies people rely on every day.

As computing continues to evolve, algorithms will play an even greater role in shaping the future. Advances in artificial intelligence, data science, and automation will depend on increasingly sophisticated algorithms capable of analyzing complex information and supporting human decision-making.

By studying how algorithms are applied across industries, students gain a broader perspective on the importance of algorithmic thinking. These systems demonstrate how structured problem-solving methods can be used to address real-world challenges and improve efficiency across many areas of society.

Ultimately, algorithms serve as the invisible engines that power much of the digital world. Whether guiding navigation systems, supporting medical diagnostics, or organizing information on the internet, algorithms transform raw data into useful insights that help individuals and organizations make informed decisions.

Chapter 14 Summary

Chapter 14 explored how algorithms are used in real-world industries and technologies. While algorithms are often studied as theoretical concepts in computer science, they play an essential role in many systems that people rely on every day. From search engines and navigation systems to healthcare and finance, algorithms help process data, solve problems, and support decision-making.

The chapter explained that search engines use algorithms to analyze billions of webpages and rank results according to relevance. Navigation systems rely on algorithms to evaluate traffic conditions and determine the fastest route to a destination. These systems must process large amounts of data quickly in order to provide useful information to users.

Financial institutions also depend on algorithms to manage transactions, detect fraud, and analyze financial markets. Fraud detection algorithms examine patterns of financial activity and identify unusual behavior that may indicate unauthorized transactions. In healthcare, algorithms help doctors analyze medical images and identify possible health risks using patient data.

The chapter also discussed the use of algorithms in education, retail, and communication technologies. Educational platforms use algorithms to personalize learning experiences, while online stores use algorithms to recommend products based on customer preferences. Social media platforms rely on algorithms to organize content and determine which posts appear in a user's feed.

In addition, algorithms are widely used in logistics, scientific research, robotics, and artificial intelligence systems. These technologies rely on algorithms to analyze data, optimize processes, and automate complex tasks. As computing technology continues to evolve, algorithms will play an even greater role in supporting innovation across many industries.

Understanding the real-world applications of algorithms helps students recognize that computer science concepts have practical value in many areas of society. These systems demonstrate how structured problem-solving methods can improve efficiency and support technological progress.

Reflection Questions

1. Why are algorithms important in modern technology and industry?
2. How do search engines use algorithms to provide relevant results?
3. In what ways do algorithms help improve efficiency in transportation and navigation systems?
4. How are algorithms used in healthcare and financial systems?
5. Why is it important to consider ethical responsibility when algorithms influence real-world decisions?

Worksheet: Algorithms in the Real World

Part A: Key Terms

Write a short explanation for each term.

1. Search algorithm
2. Recommendation system
3. Fraud detection algorithm
4. Navigation algorithm
5. Artificial intelligence system

Part B: Understanding Applications

Answer the following questions.

1. Why must search engines use efficient algorithms to process large numbers of webpages?
2. How do navigation systems use data to determine the best travel route?
3. Why do online stores use algorithms to recommend products to customers?

Part C: Industry Examples

Explain how algorithms are used in the following situations.

1. A healthcare system analyzing medical images to detect diseases.
2. A delivery company planning efficient shipping routes.
3. A music streaming platform recommending songs to listeners.

Chapter 14 Quiz

1. What technology uses algorithms to organize and rank webpages in response to user queries?

A. Search engine
B. Printer
C. Calculator
D. Monitor

2. What system uses algorithms to determine the fastest driving route?

A. Navigation system
B. Email system
C. Camera system
D. Storage system

3. What type of algorithm helps banks identify unusual financial activity?

A. Navigation algorithm
B. Fraud detection algorithm
C. Sorting algorithm
D. Translation algorithm

4. What technology uses algorithms to recommend products or content based on user behavior?

A. Recommendation system
B. Power supply
C. Input device
D. Display system

5. In which field do algorithms help analyze medical images and patient data?

A. Education
B. Healthcare
C. Agriculture
D. Architecture

Quiz Answer Key

1. A — Search engine
2. A — Navigation system
3. B — Fraud detection algorithm
4. A — Recommendation system
5. B — Healthcare

Chapter 15: The Future of Algorithms — Innovation, Challenges, and Human Responsibility

As technology continues to evolve, algorithms will play an increasingly important role in shaping the future of society. Algorithms already influence many aspects of daily life, from communication and transportation to healthcare and education. As computing systems become more powerful and data becomes more abundant, the capabilities of algorithms will continue to expand.

One of the most significant developments in recent years has been the growth of artificial intelligence and machine learning. These technologies rely on algorithms that can learn from data and improve their performance over time. In the future, algorithms will likely become even more sophisticated, allowing computers to analyze complex problems and assist humans in making better decisions.

For example, researchers are developing algorithms that can help doctors diagnose diseases earlier and more accurately. By analyzing medical images, patient histories, and genetic information, these systems may help identify health risks that might otherwise go unnoticed. In the field of environmental science, algorithms are being used to analyze climate data and model potential solutions for reducing environmental impact.

Transportation systems are also expected to change as algorithms continue to advance. Autonomous vehicles rely on algorithms to interpret sensor data, detect obstacles, and navigate safely through traffic. As these technologies improve, they may help reduce accidents, improve traffic efficiency, and transform how people travel.

Another area where algorithms will play a major role is scientific discovery. Researchers use algorithms to analyze enormous datasets generated by experiments and simulations. In fields such as astronomy, genetics, and particle physics, algorithms help scientists detect patterns and make discoveries that would be impossible to achieve manually.

Quantum computing may also influence the future of algorithms. Quantum computers operate differently from classical computers and may eventually solve certain types of problems much faster than traditional systems. Although this technology is still in development, researchers are already designing new algorithms specifically suited for quantum computing environments.

As algorithms become more powerful, they also present new challenges. One challenge involves managing the enormous volumes of data required by modern computing systems. Data storage, processing speed, and energy consumption are all important factors that must be considered when designing large-scale algorithmic systems.

Another challenge involves ensuring fairness and transparency in algorithmic decision-making. As algorithms are used in more areas of society, it becomes increasingly important to understand how these systems operate and how they affect people's lives. Developers must carefully design systems that avoid bias and treat individuals fairly.

Privacy and security will also remain major concerns in the future of algorithm development. Many digital systems collect large amounts of personal data in order to provide personalized services. Protecting this information from misuse or unauthorized access will continue to be an important responsibility for organizations and developers.

Human oversight will remain essential even as algorithms become more advanced. Although algorithms can process data quickly and identify patterns efficiently, they do not possess human judgment or ethical reasoning. Humans must therefore remain responsible for guiding how these systems are designed and used.

Education will play an important role in preparing future generations to work with algorithms responsibly. Students who understand how algorithms function will be better equipped to evaluate technology critically and contribute to its development. Algorithmic literacy will become an increasingly valuable skill as digital technologies continue to shape society.

In addition to technical knowledge, future developers will need strong ethical awareness. Designing algorithms that are fair, transparent, and secure requires thoughtful consideration of social impacts. Responsible innovation helps ensure that technological progress benefits society as a whole.

Collaboration across disciplines will also be important for the future of algorithms. Engineers, scientists, policymakers, and educators must work together to address the challenges and opportunities created by advanced technologies. By combining technical expertise with social insight, society can guide the development of algorithms in positive directions.

Despite the challenges, the future of algorithms holds tremendous promise. Algorithms will continue to support advances in medicine, environmental protection, scientific research, and many other fields. These technologies have the potential to improve quality of life and expand human knowledge in ways that were once unimaginable.

Understanding the future of algorithms helps students see how the principles they are learning today will influence tomorrow's technologies. The foundational ideas of algorithm design—such as logical reasoning, efficiency, and structured problem solving—will continue to guide innovation in computing.

Ultimately, algorithms are tools created by humans to help solve problems and organize information. Their impact depends on how thoughtfully they are designed and how responsibly they are applied. By combining technical skill with ethical awareness, future generations can ensure that algorithms remain powerful tools for progress, discovery, and human advancement.

Chapter 15 Summary

Chapter 15 explored the future of algorithms and their growing influence on society. As computing technology continues to advance, algorithms are becoming more powerful and are being used in many important fields such as healthcare, transportation, scientific research, and environmental studies. These systems help analyze large datasets, detect patterns, and assist humans in solving complex problems.

The chapter explained that artificial intelligence and machine learning will continue to play a major role in the future of algorithms. These technologies allow algorithms to learn from data and improve their performance over time. AI systems are already being used to assist doctors in diagnosing diseases, support transportation systems such as autonomous vehicles, and analyze environmental data to better understand climate patterns.

Another emerging area discussed in the chapter is quantum computing. Quantum computers operate differently from traditional computers and may allow certain types of algorithms to solve extremely complex problems much faster than current systems. Although quantum technology is still developing, researchers are already designing algorithms that could work with these future computing systems.

The chapter also highlighted several important challenges associated with the growing use of algorithms. These challenges include managing large volumes of data, ensuring fairness in algorithmic decision-making, protecting privacy, and maintaining strong cybersecurity protections. As algorithms become more integrated into society, these issues must be addressed carefully.

Human responsibility remains an essential part of the future of algorithms. Although algorithms can process information quickly, they do not possess human judgment or ethical reasoning. Developers, organizations, and policymakers must guide how these systems are designed and used.

Finally, the chapter emphasized the importance of education and algorithm literacy. Students who understand how algorithms work will be better prepared to evaluate technology, contribute to innovation, and design systems that serve society responsibly. The future of algorithms depends not only on technical advances but also on the ethical and responsible choices made by the people who develop and use them.

Reflection Questions

1. Why will algorithms continue to play an important role in the future of technology?
2. How might artificial intelligence improve decision-making in fields such as healthcare or transportation?
3. What is quantum computing, and how might it influence future algorithms?
4. Why are privacy and security important considerations in algorithm design?
5. Why must humans remain responsible for guiding how algorithms are developed and used?

Worksheet: The Future of Algorithms

Part A: Key Terms

Write a short explanation for each term.

1. Artificial Intelligence
2. Machine Learning
3. Quantum Computing
4. Algorithmic Fairness
5. Algorithm Literacy

Part B: Understanding Future Technologies

Answer the following questions.

1. How might algorithms help improve healthcare in the future?
2. Why are large datasets important for modern algorithm development?
3. Why is human oversight important even when algorithms are very advanced?

Part C: Real-World Thinking

Explain how future algorithms might help in the following situations.

1. Predicting severe weather or climate patterns.
2. Supporting self-driving vehicles.
3. Assisting scientists in analyzing complex research data.

Chapter 15 Quiz

1. What technology allows algorithms to learn patterns from data and improve performance over time?

A. Artificial Intelligence
B. Mechanical Engineering
C. Graphic Design
D. Circuit Assembly

2. What emerging computing technology may allow certain problems to be solved much faster than traditional computers?

A. Optical networking
B. Quantum computing
C. Satellite computing
D. Magnetic storage

3. Why is human oversight important in algorithm development?

A. Algorithms cannot store data
B. Algorithms do not possess human judgment or ethics
C. Algorithms cannot perform calculations
D. Algorithms cannot access networks

4. What term describes ensuring that algorithms treat individuals and groups fairly?

A. Algorithmic fairness
B. Data compression
C. Signal processing
D. Binary encoding

5. What concept refers to understanding how algorithms work and how they affect society?

A. Algorithm literacy
B. Hardware scaling
C. System formatting
D. Data routing

Quiz Answer Key

1. A — Artificial Intelligence
2. B — Quantum computing
3. B — Algorithms do not possess human judgment or ethics
4. A — Algorithmic fairness
5. A — Algorithm literacy

Chapter 16: Algorithmic Thinking — A Skill for the Future

Throughout this book, algorithms have been presented as structured procedures that guide computers in solving problems. However, the importance of algorithms extends beyond computer programming. The ability to think algorithmically—breaking problems into logical steps, evaluating possible solutions, and organizing processes efficiently—is a valuable skill that can be applied in many areas of life and work.

Algorithmic thinking refers to the process of approaching problems in a systematic and logical way. Instead of attempting to solve a complex problem all at once, algorithmic thinking encourages individuals to divide the problem into smaller, manageable steps. Each step contributes to the overall solution, creating a clear pathway from the initial problem to the final result.

This approach is not limited to computer science. People naturally use algorithmic thinking in many everyday activities. When preparing a meal, following a recipe involves completing a series of ordered steps. When planning a trip, a person might consider transportation options, travel time, and necessary preparations. In each case, the task is completed by following a sequence of logical steps.

In computing, algorithmic thinking is essential because computers rely on precise instructions. Programmers must carefully design algorithms that clearly define each step required to complete a task. If instructions are incomplete or ambiguous, the computer may produce incorrect results or fail to execute the program successfully.

Algorithmic thinking also involves evaluating efficiency and exploring alternative solutions. Often, there are multiple ways to solve the same problem. By comparing different approaches, developers can determine which method is most effective. This process encourages analytical reasoning and creative problem-solving.

Another important aspect of algorithmic thinking is abstraction. Abstraction involves focusing on the essential elements of a problem while ignoring unnecessary details. By identifying the most important components, programmers can design algorithms that address the core aspects of a task without being overwhelmed by complexity.

For example, when designing a navigation system, developers must focus on key factors such as distance, traffic conditions, and route options. Many other details—such as the color of vehicles or the architecture of nearby buildings—are not relevant to the algorithm's purpose. Abstraction helps programmers concentrate on the information that truly matters.

Pattern recognition is another skill closely related to algorithmic thinking. Many problems share similarities with other problems that have been solved before. By recognizing patterns, developers can apply existing solutions or adapt known algorithms to new situations. This ability helps reduce development time and improve efficiency.

Algorithmic thinking also encourages careful testing and refinement. Once an algorithm has been designed, it must be tested under different conditions to ensure that it works correctly. Testing helps identify errors, improve performance, and ensure that the algorithm produces reliable results.

As technology continues to advance, algorithmic thinking will become increasingly important in many professions. Fields such as engineering, data science, healthcare, finance, and environmental science rely on structured problem-solving methods to analyze information and develop solutions. Individuals who understand algorithmic thinking will be better prepared to contribute to these fields.

Education systems around the world are increasingly recognizing the importance of computational thinking and algorithmic reasoning. Teaching students how to analyze problems logically and design step-by-step solutions helps develop critical thinking skills that extend far beyond programming.

Algorithmic thinking also helps individuals evaluate technology more effectively. In a world where algorithms influence search results, social media feeds, and automated decisions, understanding how algorithms operate allows people to interact with technology more responsibly and thoughtfully.

The study of algorithms ultimately reflects a broader principle of problem solving: complex challenges can often be addressed by organizing information, applying logical reasoning, and following structured processes. These principles apply not only to computing but to many aspects of human activity.

As students reach the end of this book, they have explored many fundamental concepts related to algorithms. They have learned how algorithms organize data, search for information, make decisions, and support artificial intelligence systems. These concepts provide a foundation for understanding how modern digital technologies operate.

The future will bring new challenges and opportunities that require thoughtful problem solving. Algorithmic thinking provides tools that help individuals analyze situations, design effective solutions, and evaluate the impact of technology on society.

Ultimately, algorithms are more than technical procedures used by computers. They represent a way of thinking about problems and solutions in a structured and logical manner. By developing algorithmic thinking skills, students gain valuable tools for understanding the digital world and participating in the technological innovations that will shape the future.

Chapter 16 Summary

Chapter 16 explored the concept of algorithmic thinking and why it is an important skill for the future. While algorithms are often associated with computer programming, the structured thinking used to design them can be applied to many real-world situations. Algorithmic thinking involves breaking complex problems into smaller steps, organizing those steps logically, and working toward a clear solution.

The chapter explained that algorithmic thinking helps individuals approach challenges in a systematic and organized way. Instead of attempting to solve a complicated problem all at once, algorithmic reasoning encourages people to divide tasks into manageable parts. This process improves clarity and allows solutions to be developed step by step.

Several related concepts were discussed, including abstraction, pattern recognition, and problem decomposition. Abstraction allows individuals to focus on the most important elements of a problem while ignoring unnecessary details. Pattern recognition helps identify similarities between problems, allowing previously developed solutions to be reused or adapted. Decomposition involves dividing large problems into smaller pieces that are easier to solve.

The chapter also emphasized the importance of testing and refining algorithms. Even well-designed algorithms must be evaluated under different conditions to ensure they function correctly and efficiently. Through testing and improvement, developers strengthen the reliability of the systems they create.

In addition, the chapter highlighted the growing importance of algorithmic thinking across many professional fields. Engineers, scientists, healthcare professionals, and business analysts all rely on structured reasoning to analyze data and develop solutions. As digital technologies continue to expand, algorithmic thinking will become an increasingly valuable skill.

Finally, the chapter emphasized that algorithms are tools created by humans to solve problems. Understanding how algorithms work helps individuals interact with technology more responsibly and critically. By learning algorithmic thinking, students gain a foundation for understanding the digital world and contributing to future technological innovation.

Reflection Questions

1. What does algorithmic thinking mean, and why is it important?
2. How can breaking a complex problem into smaller steps make it easier to solve?
3. Why is abstraction useful when designing algorithms?
4. How does pattern recognition help developers solve problems more efficiently?
5. Why is algorithmic thinking considered a valuable skill for many future careers?

Worksheet: Practicing Algorithmic Thinking

Part A: Key Concepts

Write a short explanation for each term.

1. Algorithmic thinking
2. Decomposition
3. Abstraction
4. Pattern recognition
5. Testing and refinement

Part B: Problem Solving

Answer the following questions.

1. Why do programmers divide complex problems into smaller steps when designing algorithms?
2. How can recognizing patterns help improve problem-solving efficiency?
3. Why is it important to test algorithms before using them in real systems?

Part C: Everyday Algorithms

Describe how algorithmic thinking could be used in the following situations.

1. Planning a daily schedule for school activities.
2. Organizing books in a library by category.
3. Preparing a recipe by following a sequence of steps.

Chapter 16 Quiz

1. What term describes the process of solving problems using logical, step-by-step reasoning?

A. Algorithmic thinking
B. Data storage
C. Hardware engineering
D. Circuit design

2. What concept refers to breaking a complex problem into smaller parts?

A. Compression
B. Decomposition
C. Encryption
D. Compilation

3. What concept allows developers to focus on important details while ignoring unnecessary information?

A. Abstraction
B. Duplication
C. Conversion
D. Expansion

4. What skill helps developers identify similarities between different problems?

A. Data encryption
B. Pattern recognition
C. Hardware assembly
D. Signal processing

5. Why is testing important when developing algorithms?

A. To improve appearance
B. To ensure the algorithm works correctly
C. To increase file size
D. To reduce memory capacity

Quiz Answer Key

1. A — Algorithmic thinking
2. B — Decomposition
3. A — Abstraction
4. B — Pattern recognition
5. B — To ensure the algorithm works correctly

AI Glossary —

Letter A

Activation Function

A key part of neural networks that decides whether a neuron should be "activated" or not. It helps the network handle complex patterns, turning raw numbers into meaningful signals during learning.

Algorithm

A step-by-step set of instructions that tells a computer how to solve a problem or perform a task. In AI, algorithms are the "recipes" that guide machines in recognizing patterns, learning from data, and making predictions.

Anomaly Detection

A technique used in AI to find unusual patterns or behaviors that don't fit expected data. It's commonly used in fraud detection, cybersecurity, and system monitoring to identify potential problems

Artificial Intelligence (AI)

The science of creating machines that can perform tasks that normally require human intelligence — such as understanding language, recognizing images, solving problems, or making decisions.

Artificial Neural Network (ANN)

A system inspired by how the human brain works, made up of layers of connected nodes (neurons). Each node processes information and passes it along, allowing the system to "learn" patterns from data.

Artificial General Intelligence (AGI)

A theoretical form of AI that would be able to understand, learn, and perform any intellectual task a human can do. AGI doesn't exist yet, but it represents the ultimate goal of AI research — true human-like intelligence.

Artificial Narrow Intelligence (ANI)

AI designed for a specific task, such as language translation, facial recognition, or driving a car. Most AI today is narrow — powerful at one thing, but unable to perform unrelated tasks.

Attention Mechanism

A method used in advanced AI models (like transformers) that allows the system to focus on the most relevant parts of the input. It helps the AI "pay attention" to important words or data points when generating responses.

Augmented Intelligence

AI systems designed not to replace humans, but to assist them. Augmented intelligence emphasizes collaboration — combining human creativity and judgment with machine speed and accuracy.

Autonomous System

A system that can operate, make decisions, or take actions without direct human control. Examples include self-driving cars, delivery drones, or robotic assistants that use AI to navigate and respond to their environment.

Letter B

Backpropagation

A key learning process used in neural networks to adjust the model's internal settings (weights) based on the errors it makes. By "propagating" mistakes backward through the network, the AI learns to improve accuracy over time.

Batch Learning

A method where an AI model is trained on a complete dataset all at once, rather than learning continuously. It's efficient for large, static datasets but less adaptable to changing data over time.

Bayesian Network

A graphical model that represents the relationships between variables and their probabilities. It helps AI systems reason under uncertainty — for example, predicting the likelihood of an event based on known factors.

Behavioral Analytics

AI techniques that analyze user actions, preferences, or digital patterns to predict future behavior. Often used in marketing, fraud detection, and personalized recommendations.

Bias in AI

When an AI system produces unfair or unbalanced results due to biased data or flawed training methods. Bias can affect hiring systems, loan approvals, and facial recognition — making fairness testing essential in AI development.

Big Data

Extremely large and complex datasets that traditional computers can't easily process. AI tools use big data to learn patterns, make predictions, and uncover insights across industries like healthcare, finance, and marketing.

Binary Classification

A machine learning task where the AI must choose between two possible outcomes — such as "spam or not spam," "yes or no," or "disease or no disease." It's one of the most basic types of AI decision-making.

Bit

The smallest unit of digital data, representing a value of **0** or **1**. In AI and computing, bits form the foundation for all data processing, storage, and communication. Eight bits make up one **byte**, and together they represent everything from numbers and text to images and videos.

Bitwise Operation

A type of mathematical operation that works directly on the binary representation (bits) of data. Bitwise operators (such as AND, OR, XOR, and NOT) are used in AI programming to control low-level logic, optimize performance, and manipulate data efficiently.

Blockchain AI

The combination of blockchain (a secure, distributed ledger) and artificial intelligence to improve transparency, data security, and trust in AI-driven systems.

Bot

Short for "robot," a bot is a program that performs automated tasks. In AI, chatbots are designed to simulate human conversation, while other bots perform repetitive digital actions like data scraping or scheduling.

Brute Force Algorithm

A simple but computationally expensive problem-solving method that tries every possible solution until it finds the correct one. Though inefficient, it guarantees accuracy for small problems.

Letter C

Chatbot

An AI-powered program designed to simulate human conversation through text or voice. Chatbots can answer questions, provide customer support, teach lessons, or help automate business communication using natural language processing.

Classification

A core machine learning task where AI assigns input data into specific categories or labels — such as identifying whether an email is "spam" or "not spam." Classification models are trained using labeled examples to recognize patterns.

Clustering

An unsupervised learning technique where AI groups similar pieces of data together based on shared characteristics. Unlike classification, clustering doesn't use labeled data — it helps uncover hidden patterns or natural groupings within datasets.

Cognitive Computing

A branch of AI that mimics human reasoning, perception, and decision-making. Cognitive systems analyze unstructured data, recognize language and emotions, and provide intelligent suggestions — much like how the human brain interprets information.

Computer Vision

A field of AI that enables machines to "see" and interpret visual information such as images or videos. Computer vision powers facial recognition, object detection, medical imaging, and autonomous vehicles.

Convolutional Neural Network (CNN)

A specialized type of neural network used primarily for image and video analysis. CNNs automatically detect visual features like edges, shapes, and textures, allowing machines to recognize objects or patterns with high accuracy.

Context Window

The range of text or tokens that a language model can "see" and use at one time to generate its response. A larger context window allows AI to remember more of the conversation, leading to better understanding and consistency.

Corpus

A large and structured collection of texts used to train or evaluate language models. In AI, a corpus provides the examples that teach the model how words and phrases are used in real-world contexts.

Cross-Validation

A model evaluation technique used in machine learning to test how well a model generalizes to new, unseen data. The dataset is divided into parts (folds), and the model is trained and tested multiple times to ensure accuracy and reliability.

Cybernetics

The interdisciplinary study of communication and control in both machines and living organisms. In AI, cybernetics explores feedback loops — how systems monitor and adjust their behavior to maintain balance and achieve goals.

Letter D

Data Analytics

The process of examining, cleaning, and interpreting data to uncover useful information and patterns. In AI, data analytics helps models learn from real-world data to make predictions and informed decisions.

Data Labeling

The act of tagging or annotating raw data with meaningful labels — such as identifying images with "cat" or "dog." Labeled data is essential for training supervised machine learning models.

Data Mining

The practice of exploring large datasets to discover hidden patterns, trends, or relationships. AI-powered data mining helps businesses predict customer behavior, detect fraud, and improve decision-making.

Data Science

An interdisciplinary field that combines statistics, programming, and AI to extract insights from data. Data scientists build predictive models, analyze trends, and guide data-driven decisions.

Dataset

A structured collection of data used to train or test AI models. A dataset can include text, images, numbers, or audio. The quality and diversity of the dataset directly affect how well an AI performs.

Decision Tree

A visual and logical model used in AI for decision-making. Each branch represents a question or condition, and each leaf represents an outcome. Decision trees are popular for their simplicity and interpretability.

Deep Learning

A subset of machine learning that uses multi-layered neural networks to learn complex patterns. Deep learning powers technologies like voice recognition, autonomous driving, and image generation.

Dimensionality Reduction

A mathematical process used to simplify datasets by reducing the number of variables while preserving important information. It helps AI models work faster and more efficiently, especially with large data.

Domain Adaptation

A technique in AI that allows a model trained on one dataset to perform well on a different but related dataset. It helps AI generalize better to new environments or data types.

Drift Detection

The process of identifying when an AI model's performance declines because real-world data has changed. Detecting data drift ensures the model stays accurate and up-to-date over time.

Letter E

E-book Recommendation Systems

AI algorithms that suggest books or reading materials based on user preferences, past selections, or browsing behavior. They enhance reading platforms by delivering personalized content to readers.

E-Brainstorming

The use of AI tools to assist with creative idea generation. E-brainstorming platforms help individuals and teams generate fresh perspectives, organize thoughts, and develop new solutions quickly.

E-commerce AI

AI applications that enhance online shopping experiences. These systems recommend products, predict customer behavior, optimize pricing, and improve inventory management for e-commerce platforms.

Edge AI

Artificial Intelligence that runs directly on local devices (like smartphones, cameras, or IoT sensors) instead of relying on cloud servers. Edge AI allows faster responses, improved privacy, and reduced internet dependency.

E-Learning AI

The use of AI in online education to personalize learning experiences, analyze student performance, and recommend tailored study materials. E-Learning AI helps teachers and learners adapt lessons to individual needs.

E-mail Filtering AI

AI systems that automatically detect and organize incoming emails — such as sorting spam, prioritizing important messages, or detecting phishing threats — using natural language and pattern recognition.

Embedding

A mathematical representation of data (like words, sentences, or images) in numerical form. In AI, embeddings help models understand meaning, context, and similarity — crucial for natural language processing and image recognition.

Emotion AI

Also called Affective Computing, it's a branch of AI that recognizes, interprets, and responds to human emotions using facial expressions, voice tones, or physiological signals. It's used in customer service, education, and healthcare.

Ensemble Learning

A technique that combines multiple AI models to produce stronger, more accurate results than a single model could achieve alone. Common ensemble methods include bagging, boosting, and stacking.

E-Transaction Security

AI-based systems that monitor and protect online financial transactions. They detect unusual activity, verify identities, and prevent fraud in digital banking and online payment systems.

Letter F

Face Recognition AI

A technology that uses machine learning and computer vision to identify or verify a person's identity based on facial features. It's used in security systems, smartphones, and law enforcement, but also raises privacy and ethical concerns.

False Positive

A situation in which an AI system incorrectly identifies something as true when it's not. For example, a spam filter marking a legitimate email as spam. Reducing false positives improves reliability and user trust.

False Negative

The opposite of a false positive — when an AI system fails to identify something that is true. For example, a medical AI missing signs of a disease. Balancing false positives and negatives is vital in sensitive applications.

Feature Engineering

The process of creating, transforming, or selecting data features to improve machine learning model performance. It's a key step that combines human insight with data science techniques to optimize accuracy.

Feature Extraction

The process of identifying the most important characteristics or variables from raw data. In AI, feature extraction helps reduce complexity and improve model accuracy by focusing on relevant information.

Feature Map

In deep learning, particularly in convolutional neural networks (CNNs), a feature map represents visual patterns detected in an image. It helps the network recognize shapes, textures, and other important details.

Federated Learning

A training method that allows multiple devices or organizations to collaboratively train an AI model without sharing raw data. Each participant trains the model locally, and only updates are shared — improving data privacy and security.

Fine-Tuning

A process of retraining a pre-trained AI model on a smaller, specific dataset to make it more accurate for a particular task. Fine-tuning allows developers to customize general-purpose models for specialized applications.

Forecasting Model

An AI system that predicts future events or trends based on historical data. Forecasting models are widely used in business, weather prediction, finance, and supply chain management.

Fuzzy Logic

An AI reasoning system that allows for partial truths rather than strict "true or false" decisions. It's useful for handling uncertainty in real-world situations like temperature control, medical diagnosis, and robotics.

Letter G

GAN (Generative Adversarial Network)

A type of deep learning model with two neural networks — a **generator** and a **discriminator** — that work against each other. The generator creates data (like images or text), while the discriminator evaluates it for authenticity. This competition helps the model generate highly realistic outputs such as AI-generated art or photos.

General AI (Artificial General Intelligence)

A theoretical form of AI capable of understanding, learning, and applying knowledge across multiple domains — much like a human being. Unlike narrow AI, General AI could perform any intellectual task without specific training.

Genetic Algorithm

An optimization technique inspired by natural selection. It uses processes like mutation, crossover, and selection to evolve solutions to complex problems — often used in robotics, scheduling, and engineering design.

Geospatial AI

The combination of artificial intelligence with geographic data (maps, satellite images, or GPS data) to analyze spatial patterns. It's used in urban planning, agriculture, environmental monitoring, and disaster management.

Gesture Recognition

A branch of computer vision that interprets human movements — such as hand waves or facial expressions — as commands. It's commonly used in gaming, virtual reality, and touchless interfaces.

GPT (Generative Pre-trained Transformer)

A family of large language models developed by OpenAI. GPT models are trained on vast text datasets and can generate human-like text, write essays, code, or answer questions — forming the foundation for conversational AI systems like ChatGPT.

Gradient Descent

An optimization algorithm used in training neural networks. It minimizes the model's prediction error by gradually adjusting weights in the direction of the steepest decrease in loss — similar to rolling downhill to find the lowest point.

Graph Neural Network (GNN)

A type of neural network designed to process data structured as graphs — with nodes (points) and edges (connections). GNNs are used in recommendation systems, molecule analysis, and social network modeling.

Ground Truth

The real, verified data used to measure how accurate an AI model's predictions are. For example, in image recognition, the "ground truth" is the actual label of what the image shows. It's essential for evaluating model performance.

Guided Learning

An AI-assisted educational approach that provides learners with personalized hints, explanations, and progress tracking. Guided learning uses data analytics and adaptive models to support student growth in real time.

Letter H

Hallucination (in AI)

A phenomenon where an AI model generates information that appears confident and factual but is actually incorrect or fabricated. Hallucinations occur when the model fills gaps in knowledge or misinterprets data. Managing them requires clear prompts, human review, and fact-checking.

Heuristic Algorithm

A problem-solving method that uses experience-based shortcuts to find good — though not always perfect — solutions quickly. Heuristic algorithms are common in AI search systems, decision-making, and optimization problems where speed matters more than precision.

Hidden Layer

A layer of neurons in a neural network that processes inputs between the input and output layers. Hidden layers extract complex patterns from data and enable the network to make accurate predictions or classifications.

Human-Computer Interaction (HCI)

The study and design of how people interact with computers and AI systems. HCI focuses on usability, accessibility, and user experience, ensuring that AI tools feel intuitive and supportive to human users.

Human-in-the-Loop (HITL)

An AI training or decision process that includes active human participation. Humans review, correct, or guide the AI's outputs to ensure quality, fairness, and ethical alignment — especially important in high-stakes fields like healthcare and law.

Hybrid AI

An approach that combines two or more types of AI — such as symbolic reasoning (rule-based) and machine learning (data-driven) — to create systems that are both interpretable and powerful. Hybrid AI blends logic with learning for smarter, explainable outcomes.

Hyperparameter

A setting or configuration that controls how an AI model learns, such as learning rate, batch size, or number of layers. Unlike model parameters learned automatically, hyperparameters are manually chosen to optimize training performance.

Hyperparameter Tuning

The process of finding the best hyperparameter values for a model. It's often done through techniques like grid search, random search, or Bayesian optimization to achieve the highest accuracy possible.

Hypothesis Testing (in AI)

A statistical method for evaluating whether a pattern or relationship found by an AI model is real or due to chance. It helps ensure that model results are meaningful and scientifically valid.

Hybrid Cloud AI

A cloud computing setup that uses both private and public cloud environments to train and deploy AI models. It offers flexibility, scalability, and stronger control over sensitive data.

Letter I

Image Recognition

A branch of computer vision that enables AI systems to identify and categorize objects, people, or scenes in images. It's used in facial recognition, medical imaging, self-driving cars, and quality control in manufacturing.

Imbalanced Data

A situation where some classes or categories in a dataset have many more examples than others. Imbalanced data can cause AI models to favor the majority class, leading to inaccurate predictions. Balancing data improves fairness and performance.

Inference Engine

A component of an AI system that applies logical rules or learned patterns to reach conclusions or make decisions. Inference engines are core parts of expert systems and modern language models that generate intelligent responses.

Information Retrieval

The process of searching, extracting, and ranking relevant data from large datasets or documents. AI-powered search engines and chatbots use information retrieval to deliver accurate, context-aware answers.

Input Data

The raw information — such as text, numbers, or images — that an AI system receives before processing. The quality of input data directly affects the reliability of the model's output.

Intelligent Agent

A software entity capable of perceiving its environment, making decisions, and taking actions to achieve specific goals. Examples include virtual assistants, recommendation systems, and AI tutors.

Interpretable AI

An approach to AI design focused on making model decisions understandable to humans. Interpretable AI helps users trust and verify machine-generated outcomes, especially in healthcare, finance, and law.

Iterative Learning

A process where an AI model improves through repeated cycles of training, testing, and refining. Each iteration helps the system learn from its mistakes and perform better over time.

IoT (Internet of Things) AI

AI integrated with smart devices connected through the internet. IoT AI enables objects like thermostats, watches, and appliances to learn user preferences, predict behavior, and operate autonomously.

Isolation Forest

An anomaly detection algorithm that identifies unusual data points by isolating them from the rest of the dataset. It's efficient for spotting fraud, system errors, or rare events.

Letter J

Jaccard Index

A statistical measure used to compare the similarity between two sets. In AI and machine learning, it's often used to evaluate clustering or text similarity by dividing the intersection of sets by their union.

Java (in AI)

A programming language often used in AI applications due to its portability, scalability, and strong memory management. Java supports frameworks like Deeplearning4j and Weka, which help in building AI systems for enterprise and academic use.

Joint Embedding

A technique where two or more types of data — such as text and images — are represented in a shared vector space. Joint embeddings allow AI to link visual and textual understanding, as seen in models like CLIP that connect words to images.

JSON (JavaScript Object Notation)

A lightweight data format used for storing and exchanging structured information between systems. AI tools often use JSON to send model inputs, outputs, and metadata in a clear and readable way.

Jump Learning

An advanced learning concept where AI "jumps ahead" in reasoning or skill based on prior knowledge, instead of learning everything from scratch. It mimics human intuition and helps reduce training time in complex models.

Letter K

Keyword Extraction

A natural language processing technique used to identify the most relevant words or phrases within text. It helps summarize content, improve search results, and enhance AI-driven document classification.

Kernel Function

A mathematical function used in Support Vector Machines (SVMs) to transform data into a higher-dimensional space. This allows the AI to separate complex, non-linear data more effectively. Common kernel types include linear, polynomial, and radial basis functions.

Kinetic AI

A branch of AI that studies movement and motion analysis. It's used in robotics, sports technology, and autonomous vehicles to understand physical actions and predict motion patterns.

K-Means Clustering

An unsupervised learning algorithm that divides data into K distinct groups based on similarity. It assigns each data point to the cluster with the nearest mean value. K-Means is widely used in customer segmentation, image compression, and pattern recognition.

K-Nearest Neighbor (KNN)

A simple yet powerful machine learning algorithm that classifies data based on its proximity to K neighboring points. It assumes similar data points are likely to have similar outcomes. KNN is used in recommendation systems and predictive analytics.

Knowledge Base

A structured collection of information that an AI system uses to answer questions, make decisions, or provide explanations. Knowledge bases power systems like virtual assistants, expert systems, and search engines.

Knowledge Distillation

A process where a smaller AI model learns from a larger, more complex model. This helps create faster, lightweight systems that maintain strong performance while using fewer computational resources.

Knowledge Graph

A network that connects information through relationships and context, enabling AI systems to understand how data points relate. Knowledge graphs are used by companies like Google to enhance search accuracy and context understanding.

Knowledge Representation

The method of encoding information in a way that AI systems can understand and use for reasoning. It includes logic rules, ontologies, and semantic networks, allowing AI to store and apply knowledge intelligently.

Knowledge Transfer

A technique in AI and machine learning where knowledge gained from one task or dataset is reused in another. This reduces the need for retraining from scratch and speeds up learning in related areas.

Letter L

Label Encoding

A data preprocessing technique used to convert categorical (text-based) values into numerical form so that AI models can process them. For example, "Red," "Green," and "Blue" may be encoded as 0, 1, and 2.

Labeled Data

Data that has been tagged with correct answers or classifications, such as images labeled "cat" or "dog." Labeled data is essential for training supervised learning models that rely on known outcomes.

Language Model

An AI system trained to understand, predict, and generate human language. It learns from massive text datasets to perform tasks like translation, summarization, and conversation — examples include GPT and Gemini.

Latent Space

A hidden mathematical representation within an AI model that captures complex relationships between data points. In generative AI, latent space allows systems to create new images, sounds, or text by exploring abstract features.

Lazy Learning

A machine learning approach where the model delays generalization until a prediction is requested. Algorithms like K-Nearest Neighbor (KNN) store data and only compute results when needed, trading speed for flexibility.

Linear Regression

A basic yet powerful algorithm that predicts outcomes by finding the best-fitting straight line through data points. It's commonly used in finance, sales forecasting, and scientific analysis.

Logistic Regression

A classification algorithm used to predict categorical outcomes (like "yes" or "no") instead of continuous values. Despite its name, it's mainly used for probability-based classification rather than regression.

Long Short-Term Memory (LSTM)

A special type of recurrent neural network (RNN) designed to remember long-term dependencies in sequential data, such as language or time series. LSTMs are used in speech recognition, translation, and text generation.

Loss Function

A mathematical formula that measures how far an AI model's predictions are from the correct answers. The goal of training is to minimize this loss, helping the model improve accuracy over time.

Low-Code AI

AI tools that allow users to build and deploy machine learning models with minimal coding. They simplify development for non-programmers, empowering educators, entrepreneurs, and small businesses to use AI effectively.

Letter M

Machine Learning (ML)

A core branch of AI where systems learn from data to make predictions or decisions without being explicitly programmed. It powers tools like recommendation engines, fraud detection, and voice recognition.

Meta Learning

Also called "learning to learn," this technique trains AI systems to adapt quickly to new tasks by using prior knowledge. Meta learning helps models generalize better with less training data.

Model Training

The process of teaching an AI model to recognize patterns by feeding it large amounts of data. During training, the model adjusts its internal parameters to minimize errors and improve predictions.

Model Evaluation

A step where an AI model's accuracy and performance are tested using data it hasn't seen before. Evaluation ensures that the model works well in real-world scenarios.

Model Overfitting

A situation where an AI model learns too closely from training data, capturing noise instead of patterns. Overfitting causes poor performance on new data. Regularization and validation help prevent it.

Model Optimization

The process of improving an AI model's efficiency, accuracy, and speed by fine-tuning its architecture, parameters, or algorithms.

Monte Carlo Simulation

A statistical method that uses random sampling to estimate outcomes in uncertain situations. AI systems use it for risk analysis, forecasting, and game simulations.

Multimodal AI

An AI system capable of understanding and processing information from multiple sources — such as text, images, sound, and video — to produce richer and more accurate results.

Multi-Agent System

A group of AI agents that work together or compete to achieve individual or shared goals. They are used in simulations, logistics, and automated trading systems.

Mutation Algorithm

A process inspired by genetics where random changes are introduced to improve AI models' performance during optimization or evolutionary learning.

Letter N

Naive Bayes Algorithm

A simple but powerful machine learning algorithm based on probability. It's widely used in spam detection, text classification, and sentiment analysis.

Named Entity Recognition (NER)

An NLP technique that identifies and classifies specific names or entities (like people, places, or organizations) within text.

Natural Language Processing (NLP)

A field of AI that enables machines to understand and respond to human language. It powers chatbots, translation tools, and voice assistants.

Natural Language Understanding (NLU)

A subset of NLP that focuses on interpreting meaning, emotion, and intent behind text or speech. It allows AI to understand context and tone.

Neural Architecture Search (NAS)

An automated method for designing neural networks. AI systems use NAS to discover optimal model structures without human intervention.

Neural Network

A computational model inspired by the human brain, made of layers of nodes (neurons) that process data. Neural networks are the foundation of deep learning systems.

Neuron

Definition

In artificial intelligence and machine learning, a **neuron** (also called a *node* or *unit*) is the fundamental building block of an artificial neural network. It is modeled loosely after the biological neuron found in the human brain. Each artificial neuron receives input signals, processes them mathematically, and produces an output that is passed to other neurons in the network. Neurons collectively enable a model to learn, recognize patterns, and make predictions by adjusting their internal parameters during training.

Key Components

1. **Inputs:**
   The data values or signals that are fed into the neuron — similar to how biological neurons receive signals through dendrites.

2. **Weights:**
   Numerical values assigned to each input that determine their importance. The neuron learns by adjusting these weights during training.
3. **Summation Function:**
   A mathematical operation that combines the weighted inputs into a single value, often using a simple addition or dot product.
4. **Activation Function:**
   A non-linear function (such as ReLU, Sigmoid, or Tanh) applied to the summation result to decide whether the neuron should "fire" or remain inactive.
5. **Output:**
   The final result produced by the neuron after applying the activation function, which becomes the input for other neurons in subsequent layers.

Benefits

- Allows complex relationships to be learned from raw data.
- Enables non-linear transformations for deep learning tasks.
- Builds scalable and flexible structures that can adapt to various problems.
- Mimics the way biological neurons communicate and adapt over time.

Disadvantages

- Individual neurons are simple and limited in function; meaningful behavior arises only when many are connected.
- May become computationally expensive as the network grows deeper.
- Can overfit data if not properly regularized.

Examples

- A neuron in a **convolutional neural network (CNN)** may detect visual patterns such as edges or textures.
- In a **language model**, neurons may learn linguistic features like word order or meaning.
- In **speech recognition**, neurons can capture tone, pitch, and pronunciation patterns.

Applications

- **Image Recognition:** Detecting and classifying objects, faces, or handwriting.
- **Natural Language Processing:** Understanding text, context, and sentiment.
- **Financial Forecasting:** Identifying market trends from numerical data.
- **Medical Diagnosis:** Interpreting scans, patterns, and patient records.

Industries Using Neuron-Based Models

- **Healthcare:** Predictive diagnosis and imaging analysis.
- **Education:** Adaptive learning and student performance prediction.
- **Technology:** AI assistants, chatbots, and autonomous systems.

- **Transportation:** Self-driving cars and sensor-based navigation.

Challenges

- Understanding neuron-level decision-making remains difficult, leading to "black box" behavior.
- Requires large amounts of data and computational resources to train effectively.
- Sensitive to data quality — poor input can lead to unreliable neuron activation.

Summary

A **neuron** is the core unit of intelligence within an artificial neural network. By processing inputs through weighted connections and activation functions, neurons enable machines to simulate learning and reasoning similar to the human brain. Though individually simple, millions of interconnected neurons together form the foundation of modern AI systems, powering technologies from image recognition to natural language understanding.

Node

A basic unit in a neural network that receives input, processes it, and sends it forward. Nodes collectively form layers that learn from data.

Noise (in Data)

Random or irrelevant information in a dataset that can confuse AI models. Removing noise improves accuracy and training efficiency.

Nonlinear Activation

A mathematical function in neural networks that allows models to learn complex, non-straight-line relationships. Common examples include ReLU, Sigmoid, and Tanh functions.

Normalization

A data preprocessing step that scales values into a consistent range to help AI models learn faster and perform better.

Letter O

Object Detection

A computer vision technique that identifies and locates objects within an image or video. It's used in autonomous driving, security systems, and retail analytics.

Objective Function

A mathematical formula that defines the goal of an AI model — usually to minimize error or maximize accuracy. It guides the learning process during training.

One-Hot Encoding

A method used to represent categorical data numerically by converting each value into a binary vector. It helps AI systems interpret text-based or labeled inputs.

Ontology (in AI)

A structured framework that defines relationships between concepts within a domain. Ontologies help AI organize knowledge logically and reason effectively.

Optimization Algorithm

A method used to adjust model parameters during training to minimize loss and improve accuracy. Examples include Gradient Descent and Adam Optimizer.

Optimization Problem

A task in AI where the goal is to find the best possible solution — like minimizing cost or maximizing performance — under certain constraints.

Outlier Detection

The process of identifying data points that deviate significantly from the rest. Outlier detection helps find errors, fraud, or anomalies.

Overfitting

When an AI model performs well on training data but fails to generalize to new data because it memorized instead of learning patterns.

Overparameterization

A condition where an AI model has more parameters than necessary, often leading to overfitting and inefficiency.

Oversampling

A data balancing technique that increases the number of examples in an underrepresented class to prevent bias during training.

Letter P

Parameter

A value inside an AI model that determines how it makes predictions. Parameters are adjusted during training to minimize error and improve accuracy.

Pattern Recognition

The ability of AI systems to identify regularities, trends, or structures in data. It's used in handwriting recognition, medical imaging, and speech analysis.

Perceptron

One of the earliest types of artificial neural networks. It consists of a single layer of nodes and is used for simple classification tasks.

Predictive Analytics

A branch of AI that uses statistical models and machine learning to forecast future events based on historical data.

Preprocessing

The preparation of data before feeding it into an AI model — including cleaning, scaling, and encoding — to ensure accuracy and consistency.

Probability Distribution

A statistical function that describes the likelihood of different outcomes in a dataset. It's essential for probabilistic reasoning and uncertainty modeling in AI.

Prompt Engineering

The practice of crafting precise and intentional instructions (prompts) to guide AI models in generating accurate and creative responses. It's the foundation of effective human-AI communication.

Probability Distribution

A statistical function that describes the likelihood of different outcomes in a dataset. It's essential for probabilistic reasoning and uncertainty modeling in AI.

Python (Programming Language)

A versatile, easy-to-learn programming language widely used in AI and data science. Python supports major libraries like TensorFlow, PyTorch, and Scikit-learn, making it the most popular tool for AI development.

Pre-trained Model

An AI model that has already been trained on large datasets and can be fine-tuned for specific tasks. Using pre-trained models saves time and computing resources.

Precision and Recall

Two key metrics for evaluating AI performance. **Precision** measures accuracy among positive predictions, while **Recall** measures how many actual positives were correctly identified.

Letter Q

Q-Learning

A type of reinforcement learning algorithm where an agent learns to make decisions by receiving rewards or penalties. It helps AI systems determine the best action to take in each situation, such as in robotics or game AI.

Quantization

A technique that reduces the precision of numbers in AI models to make them smaller and faster without major loss in accuracy. It's commonly used to optimize models for mobile or edge devices.

Quantum AI

The integration of quantum computing and artificial intelligence. Quantum AI uses the principles of quantum mechanics to process complex computations faster than traditional computers.

Query

A request for information sent to a database or AI system. In natural language models, queries are user inputs — the "questions" that trigger responses.

Queue Learning

A data-handling strategy where information is processed sequentially, one at a time. It's useful for managing AI tasks or workflows that must follow a specific order.

Letter R

Random Forest

An ensemble learning algorithm that combines multiple decision trees to improve accuracy and reduce overfitting. It's used for both classification and regression tasks.

Recurrent Neural Network (RNN)

A neural network designed for sequential data such as text, speech, or time series. RNNs have loops that allow them to "remember" previous inputs, making them ideal for language and forecasting tasks.

Regression Analysis

A statistical method that models the relationship between variables to predict future outcomes. Linear and logistic regression are common types.

Reinforcement Learning

An AI learning method where an agent interacts with its environment and learns from feedback through rewards and penalties. It's used in robotics, gaming, and automation.

Representation Learning

A machine learning technique where the system automatically discovers useful features from raw data instead of relying on manual feature selection.

Retrieval-Augmented Generation (RAG)

A model that combines information retrieval and text generation. It fetches relevant data before producing a response, improving accuracy in AI question-answering systems.

Reward Function

A key component of reinforcement learning that defines how much "reward" an AI receives for taking certain actions. It guides the system toward desirable outcomes.

Robotic Process Automation (RPA)

Technology that uses AI to automate repetitive digital tasks, such as data entry or document processing, to increase efficiency and reduce human error.

Rule-Based System

An AI system that makes decisions based on predefined rules or conditions, often used in expert systems or early AI programs.

Runtime Environment

The system or platform where AI models are executed. It includes the software, hardware, and configurations required for the model to function properly.

Letter S

Scalability

The ability of an AI system to handle increasing amounts of data or users without losing performance. Scalable AI models grow with business and computational needs.

Semi-Supervised Learning

A learning method that combines a small amount of labeled data with a large amount of unlabeled data to improve model performance.

Sentiment Analysis

A natural language processing technique that identifies emotions or opinions in text, such as positive, negative, or neutral sentiment. It's used in marketing and social media monitoring.

Signal Processing

The analysis and transformation of data signals (like sound, images, or time series) into meaningful patterns. AI uses it in speech recognition and medical imaging.

Speech Recognition

A technology that converts spoken language into text using AI models trained on voice data. It powers virtual assistants and transcription tools.

Supervised Learning

A machine learning technique where a model is trained using labeled data, meaning both inputs and correct outputs are provided during training.

Swarm Intelligence

An AI concept inspired by nature, where simple agents (like ants or bees) collectively solve complex problems. It's used in optimization, robotics, and network routing.

8. Symbolic AI

An early AI approach based on logical rules and symbolic representations. Unlike modern machine learning, it uses explicit reasoning rather than pattern recognition.

Synthetic Data

Artificially generated data created to train AI models when real data is limited or sensitive. It helps improve privacy and expand datasets.

Letter T

Target Variable

The specific outcome or label that an AI model aims to predict, such as "spam or not spam" or "disease present or absent."

TensorFlow

An open-source AI framework developed by Google that helps developers build and train machine learning models efficiently.

Token Limit

The maximum number of tokens (words or symbols) an AI model can process in a single interaction or context window

Tokenization

The process of breaking text into smaller units, or "tokens," such as words or subwords, to help AI models understand language.

Transfer Learning

A technique where a model pre-trained on one task is adapted to a different but related task, saving time and improving performance.

Transformer Architecture

Definition

Transformer Architecture is a deep learning model framework introduced in 2017 by Vaswani et al. in the paper *"Attention Is All You Need."* It revolutionized natural language processing (NLP) by replacing traditional sequence models like RNNs (Recurrent Neural Networks) and LSTMs (Long Short-Term Memory networks) with a mechanism known as **self-attention**, allowing the model to understand relationships between words or elements in a sequence — regardless of their distance from each other.

Key Components

1. **Encoder-Decoder Structure:**
   The architecture typically has two main parts — the encoder, which reads and represents the input data, and the decoder, which generates the output based on the encoded information.
2. **Self-Attention Mechanism:**
   This mechanism lets the model weigh the importance of each word relative to others in a sentence, improving context understanding.
3. **Multi-Head Attention:**
   Multiple attention layers run in parallel, enabling the model to capture different kinds of relationships or meanings simultaneously.
4. **Positional Encoding:**
   Since Transformers do not process data sequentially, positional encodings are added to indicate the order of elements in a sentence.
5. **Feed-Forward Networks:**
   After attention layers, fully connected neural networks help the model transform and refine the contextual representations.
6. **Residual Connections and Layer Normalization:**
   These ensure stability during training and help the model learn complex patterns efficiently.

Benefits

- Handles long-range dependencies more effectively than RNNs.
- Enables parallel processing, making it faster to train on large datasets.
- Produces state-of-the-art performance across multiple tasks, such as translation, summarization, and text generation.
- Scales well to massive datasets and larger models like GPT, BERT, and T5.

Disadvantages

- Extremely data- and computation-intensive, requiring powerful hardware.
- Can be prone to bias if trained on unbalanced or low-quality datasets.
- Difficult to interpret because of its complexity and multi-layered attention mechanisms.

Applications

- **Natural Language Processing (NLP):** Machine translation, text summarization, sentiment analysis, and chatbots.
- **Vision Transformers (ViTs):** Image recognition and object detection in computer vision.
- **Speech Recognition:** Improved context-aware transcription and voice command systems.
- **Multimodal AI:** Combining text, images, and audio for generative and reasoning tasks.

Industries Using Transformer Models

- **Technology:** Google, OpenAI, Meta, and Microsoft for large-scale AI systems.
- **Education:** Intelligent tutoring systems and adaptive learning platforms.
- **Healthcare:** Medical data analysis and clinical text interpretation.
- **Entertainment:** Script generation, gaming narratives, and subtitles translation.

Challenges

- High energy consumption during training and inference.
- Potential for producing inaccurate or biased outputs if the model is not fine-tuned properly.
- Data privacy concerns in large-scale, open-domain training environments.

Summary

The Transformer Architecture represents a fundamental shift in how machines understand and generate language. Its self-attention mechanism allows models to process context more globally and flexibly than ever before. Transformers laid the foundation for today's most advanced AI systems — including ChatGPT, BERT, and countless others — marking a turning point in modern artificial intelligence.

Transformer Model

A neural network architecture that processes sequences of data (like text) more efficiently than traditional RNNs. It's the foundation of modern large language models such as GPT.

Training Data

The dataset used to teach an AI model. Training data must be diverse and accurate to ensure reliable model performance.

Turing Test

A test developed by Alan Turing to evaluate whether a machine can exhibit intelligent behavior indistinguishable from that of a human.

Time Series Analysis

The use of AI to analyze sequential data over time, such as stock prices or weather patterns, to forecast future trends.

Tunable Parameters

Adjustable values in an AI model that influence its performance, such as learning rate or layer depth. Tuning helps achieve optimal results.

Letter U

Unlabeled Data

Data that has not been tagged with specific outputs or categories. It's commonly used in unsupervised and semi-supervised learning.

Unstructured Data

Information that doesn't follow a predefined format, such as text, images, videos, or social media posts. AI tools process it using natural language and computer vision techniques.

Unsupervised Learning

A machine learning method where models learn from unlabeled data to find patterns, groupings, or hidden structures without specific instructions.

Uncertainty Modeling

The process of estimating how confident an AI model is about its predictions. It helps improve trust and decision-making in sensitive domains like medicine or finance.

Update Rate

The frequency at which an AI model adjusts its parameters during training. A balanced update rate ensures faster learning without instability.

User Intent Recognition

An NLP technique that determines the purpose or goal behind a user's input — essential in chatbots and voice assistants for accurate responses.

Utility Function

A mathematical function used in AI to evaluate the desirability or usefulness of different actions. It's often used in decision-making and reinforcement learning.

Letter V

Validation Set

A portion of the dataset used during model training to fine-tune parameters and prevent overfitting. It helps evaluate how well the model generalizes to unseen data before final testing.

Value Function (in Reinforcement Learning)

A function that estimates the expected reward an AI agent will receive from a certain state or action. It guides decision-making by helping the agent choose actions that maximize long-term rewards.

Variance (in AI Models)

A measure of how much a model's predictions change when trained on different data samples. High variance means the model is sensitive to noise and may overfit.

Vectorization

The process of converting data (like text or images) into numerical vectors that AI models can process. It's essential in natural language processing and computer vision.

Verification (in AI Systems)

The process of checking whether an AI model or system performs its intended function correctly and safely before deployment.

Virtual Agent

An AI-driven digital assistant designed to interact with humans through voice or text. Examples include chatbots, customer service bots, and AI tutors.

Virtual Reality (VR)

A computer-generated environment that simulates real or imagined worlds. When combined with AI, VR can create adaptive, interactive learning and training experiences.

Vision Transformer (ViT)

A deep learning model that applies transformer architecture — originally used for language — to image recognition tasks. It divides images into patches and processes them like words in a sentence.

Voice Recognition

AI technology that identifies and processes human voices to perform tasks, such as unlocking devices or activating voice assistants.

Volumetric Data

Three-dimensional data used in fields like medical imaging, 3D modeling, and geoscience. AI uses it to analyze structures and visualize depth in complex environments.

Letter W

Weak AI (Narrow AI)

AI designed to perform a specific task, such as translation or image classification. It does not possess general reasoning or consciousness like humans.

Weight (in Neural Networks)

A numerical value that determines the strength of a connection between neurons. During training, weights are adjusted to reduce prediction errors.

Weighted Average

A statistical method that assigns different importance (weights) to data points when calculating an average. AI uses it to prioritize more relevant or reliable data.

Whisper Model

An AI model developed by OpenAI for automatic speech recognition (ASR). It transcribes and translates spoken language into text across multiple languages with high accuracy.

Wi-Fi Sensing AI

Technology that uses Wi-Fi signals to detect movement or monitor environments without cameras. It's used in security, healthcare, and smart homes.

Windowing Function

A mathematical function used in signal processing and speech recognition to divide data into smaller segments for analysis.

Word Embedding

A representation of words in numerical form where similar words are placed close together in vector space. It helps AI models understand semantic relationships in text.

Word2Vec

A popular algorithm for creating word embeddings by learning relationships between words based on their context within large text datasets.

Workflow Automation

The use of AI to streamline repetitive business tasks such as approvals, document sorting, and scheduling. It increases productivity and reduces human error.

World Model (in AI)

A conceptual model an AI system builds to understand and predict the behavior of the environment around it — especially in robotics and autonomous systems.

Letter X

XAI (Explainable AI)

A field of AI focused on making models transparent and understandable to humans. It explains how decisions are made, which builds trust and accountability.

XGBoost (Extreme Gradient Boosting)

A powerful machine learning algorithm known for its high performance in classification and regression tasks. It's widely used in data science competitions and predictive modeling.

XML (Extensible Markup Language)

A structured text format used to store and share data between systems. AI applications use XML for configuration, annotations, and data exchange.

XOR Problem

A classic logic problem that early neural networks struggled to solve. It led to the development of multilayer neural networks capable of learning non-linear relationships.

Letter Y

YAML (YAML Ain't Markup Language)

A human-readable data format often used for AI configuration files, datasets, and machine learning pipelines. It's easy to read and integrates well with Python-based AI frameworks.

Yield Prediction AI

AI systems that forecast agricultural output based on environmental data, crop type, and soil conditions. It supports smarter farming and food sustainability.

Yearly Seasonality Model

A model used in time-series forecasting that accounts for repeating annual patterns — such as sales spikes or weather cycles — to improve accuracy.

YOLO (You Only Look Once)

A fast real-time object detection algorithm that identifies and locates multiple objects in a single pass. It's widely used in autonomous vehicles and security systems.

Letter Z

Zero-Shot Learning

An AI method that allows a model to recognize new objects or tasks it has never seen before by using prior knowledge or contextual reasoning.

Zettabyte

A unit of digital storage equal to one sextillion (10^{21}) bytes. AI models and data centers increasingly operate with zettabyte-scale data due to massive global information growth.

Z-Score Normalization

A statistical technique used to standardize data by subtracting the mean and dividing by the standard deviation. It helps machine learning models handle data with different scales.

Zone-Based AI

A decision-making approach where an AI system divides its environment into regions or "zones" for localized reasoning and optimized control — used in robotics and traffic management.

Teacher Implementation Guide

Teaching Algorithms: Understanding the Invisible Logic of the Digital World

Purpose of This Guide

This guide is designed to help educators effectively integrate the book **"The Power of Algorithms: How Computers Solve Problems Step by Step"** into classroom instruction. The goal is to support teachers in introducing students to the foundational concepts of algorithms, computational thinking, and artificial intelligence in an accessible and engaging way.

Algorithms are the logical instructions that allow computers to perform tasks, solve problems, and process information. As modern society becomes increasingly dependent on digital systems, it is essential for students to understand the mechanisms behind the technologies they use every day.

This guide provides instructional strategies, discussion prompts, and learning activities that can help teachers transform algorithm concepts into meaningful learning experiences.

Course Structure Overview

The book is organized into **16 chapters**, which can easily align with a **16-week semester course** or be adapted into shorter instructional modules.

Suggested pacing:

Week	Chapter Topic
Week 1	Introduction & Chapter 1
Week 2	Chapter 2
Week 3	Chapter 3
Week 4	Chapter 4
Week 5	Chapter 5
Week 6	Chapter 6
Week 7	Chapter 7
Week 8	Chapter 8
Week 9	Chapter 9
Week 10	Chapter 10
Week 11	Chapter 11
Week 12	Chapter 12

Week	**Chapter Topic**
Week 13	Chapter 13
Week 14	Chapter 14
Week 15	Chapter 15
Week 16	Chapter 16 & Final Reflection

Teachers may adjust pacing depending on student level and available instructional time.

NOTES: